THE HIDDEN LEGACY

Uncovering, Confronting and Healing Three Generations of Incest

Barbara Small Hamilton

The Hidden Legacy
Copyright © 1992, 1997 by Barbara Small Hamilton.
All rights reserved.
Published by Cypress House, 155 Cypress, Fort Bragg, California 95437

The author wishes to thank the following authors and/or publishers for their permission to quote them and reprint from their published works:

From MEN WHO HATE WOMEN AND THE WOMEN WHO LOVE THEM by Susan Forward and Joan Torres. Copyright © 1986 by Susan Forward and Joan Torres. Used by permission of Bantam Books, a division of Bantam Doubleday Dell Publishing Group, Inc.

From OUT OF THE SHADOWS by Patrick Carnes, Ph.D. Copyright © 1983, Compcare Publishers, Minneapolis, Minnesota. (800) 328-3330. Used with permission.

From the book WOMEN WHO LOVE TOO MUCH by Robin Norwood. Copyright © 1985 by Robin Norwood. Reprinted with permission from Jeremy P. Tarcher, Inc., Los Angeles, CA.

The poem, "After A While," by Veronica A. Shoffstall. Copyright © 1971 by Veronica A. Shoffstall. Used with permission.

From OUTRAGEOUS ACTS AND EVERYDAY REBELLIONS by Gloria Steinem. Copyright © 1983 by Gloria Steinem. Copyright © 1984 by East Toledo Productions, Inc. Reprinted by courtesy of Henry Holt and Company, Inc.

From CONSPIRACY OF SILENCE by Sandra Butler. Copyright © 1978 by Sandra Butler. New Glide Publications, San Francisco. Used with permission.

From THE HUMAN ANIMAL by Phil Donahue. Copyright © 1985 by Multi media Entertainment, Inc., and Woodward/White, Inc. Reprinted by permission of Simon & Schuster.

The poem, "Even This," from OUR STUNNING HARVEST: POEMS BY ELLEN BASS, Copyright © 1985 by Ellen Bass. Published by New Society Publishers. Used with permission.

From the poem, "Remember," by Yarrow Morgan. Copyright © 1979 by Yarrow Morgan. Previously published in the magazine *Sinister Wisdom* in 1979 and in VOICES IN THE NIGHT, WOMEN SPEAKING ABOUT INCEST, Cleis Press, 1982. Used with permission.

From BLUE BELLE by Andrew Vachss. Copyright © 1988 by Andrew Vachss. Published by Alfred A. Knopf, Inc., New York. Used with permission.

From FATHER-DAUGHTER INCEST by Judith Lewis Herman. Copyright © 1981 by the President and Fellows of Harvard College. Published by Harvard University Press, Cambridge, Massachusetts. Used with permission.

From FAKE WITNESS by Dorothy Uhnak. Copyright © 1981 by Dorothy Uhnak. Reprinted by permission of Simon & Schuster.

Library of Congress Cataloging-in-Publication Data
Hamilton, Barbara Small.
   The hidden legacy : uncovering, confronting, and healing three generations of incest / Barbara Small Hamilton.
      p. cm.
   Includes bibliographical references.
   ISBN 1-879384-17-5 : $12.95
   1. Incest—United States—Case studies. 2. Incest victims—United States—Biography.
3. Incest victims—United States—Family relationships—Case studies.   I. Title.
   HV6570.7.H36 1992
   362.7'64—dc20   92-24541
                                                                                                  CIP

Cover drawing by Judith Hower. Cover design by Bruce Robinson.
Back cover photograph by Lisa Gurian.

To order audio: Hidden Legacy, PO Box 401, Pacific Grove, CA 93950
1-800-500-1020 * email:Hlegacy@aol.com
$48+$4 S/H CA, NY sales tax applicable

ACKNOWLEDGMENTS

"Somehow there's a real reluctance on the part of optimistic people like Americans to acknowledge the presence of evil."

Bill Moyers

But evil exposed must be acknowledged.

During the course of writing this book, those who assisted, guided and supported me also strengthened and deepened my commitment to expose the evil hidden in our family legacy—no matter what it took. From the beginning, one by one, they joined me with their skills, their energy, their wisdom and their hearts. They knew it was "one person's story told for all people," and they gave of themselves to help me tell it.

Sharon Zimmerman, my sensitive therapist Sarah, with whom I was "working through" my childhood when the book began and with whom I dared to share the first few pages. She was always "there" for me—even several years after our last session when she read and endorsed the completed manuscript of the book.

Ellen Bass, the writer and teacher who became my guide and friend while she assisted me with the early drafts. Her sensitive insistence on openness promoted my recovery and clarified my writing. Her support extended through her excellent workshops for women writers and for survivors of child sexual abuse.

Lucy Diggs, the writer who read and generously edited the entire second draft, then continued to critique my revisions by mail and long distance phone calls—for months.

It is impossible to draw lines between those who assisted my healing and those who assisted my writing, even though they may be publicly known in different professions. It all flowed together.

Bruce Robinson, the editor I worked with on the final drafting of the manuscript, graciously made himself available as often as necessary for the intensive, fine-tuning required to finish it.

Cynthia Frank of Cypress House guided me through the countless details of publishing with a clear focus, unending resourcefulness and gracious enthusiasm.

There are two others who, although they did not work with me on the manuscript, did read it and joined me in spirit, They are: Dan Corsello, Director of Napa County Human Services Delivery System and Sandra Butler, who wrote *Conspiracy of Silence* and whose offer of assistance I have described in the story.

Lynne, more twin-sister than friend in empathy and insights, refused to read one word of the book until it was finished, and thereby kept me going (I could hardly wait for her to read it!). She continues to share encouragement, wisdom and strength in the battle against child abuse.

Joan Rianda patiently saw me through months of re-writing and made concrete suggestions as we went along. Her insistence that I read each chapter aloud, painful for her to hear, enhanced my efforts to get well.

A number of others have read the manuscript and given me their generous and compassionate responses. Although I can't name everyone whose interest I welcomed, please know that your encouragement sustained and strengthened me every step of the way.

From the very beginning, my children and grandchildren have been supportive and patient during a seemingly endless project. They reviewed countless drafts for accuracy, while more of their own memories surfaced. Without their courage in sharing painful and heartbreaking information, the scope of this book could not have been achieved. Their unbeatable spirit and strength continue to inspire me.

"If you can face it
You can probably bear it.

If you can bear it
You can probably change it."

James Baldwin

TABLE OF CONTENTS

PART FOUR

PART FIVE

To my children and grandchildren
who made it possible
to tell it like it was.

To children everywhere
as they expose their Secrets,
ride out the storms,
and discover
they are not alone.

Our numbers are rising . . . .

FOREWORD

This is my personal story. My purpose is to tell the truth about child sexual abuse within the family and to reveal its effects as I have come to understand them. For although the years I describe are past, the effects are not; they linger to color present family relationships as each member comes to terms with what was and strives to make better what is. The observations I share and the conclusions I have reached are offered as a daughter and a mother—not as a professional.

At the outset, I want to state clearly what I mean when I use the term incest. It is not limited to the dictionary definition, "sexual intercourse between close blood relations." It includes those sexually derived actions which are inappropriate, intrusive, secretive, or from which the child feels unable to extricate herself (I use the feminine pronoun only for simplicity and because it is my story. Boys suffer enormously from sexual assaults).

Incestuous behavior may include fondling, seductive snuggling with or without arousal, genital tickling during roughhousing, masturbation and any number of sexual activities, including oral/genital contacts, between various combinations of relatives, including step-parents.

I have been encouraged to continue this project by a friend I have known for many years. She is one of many who, although they did not suffer overt sexual abuse during childhood, did endure embarrassing and annoying attentions from their fathers—a form of covert sexual abuse. Trying to deflect these supposedly innocent aggressions, masked as affection, was never successful.

The powerlessness experienced by these daughters during childhood spawned their subsequent vulnerability to abuse. They frequently feel angry but impotent in working through situations where authority and power are factors. I hope to reach some of these women who have unanswered questions about themselves as children and themselves now and offer some understanding of the forces that held us prisoner while we were growing up.

This has not been an easy book to write, but once begun I knew it had to be continued. The most difficult decision I had to make developed around the issue of one of the abusers. Would omitting the account of a self-admitted, one-time-only sexual assault diminish the integrity of the book? I must admit that I agonized over this for a long time. In the end, I found the answer by returning to my original purpose—to tell the truth and to reveal the effects as I have come to understand them.

My focus remains on the objects of my deepest concern: victims and survivors, young and old, **especially the children who could not speak for themselves.**

* * * * * * * * * * * * * * * *

PSEUDONYMS

Those who appear in these pages identified by first names only have been given pseudonyms. This includes family members and some friends.

All situations, incidents, places and events are described as accurately as possible.

B.H.

...Recently as I was lying on my back in bed,

a huge head appeared over me in the dark.
I was very small and at first I couldn't see
who it was. I held my breath in terror as
it moved down closer to my tiny face.
Suddenly, I recognized Dad, but his face was
enormous.
His eyes held mine without blinking
and he wasn't smiling. Then his lips moved.

I pressed my head into my pillow, crying out
in alarm, "Oh, no! Oh, no!"
He nearly smothered me as his face covered mine
and he kissed me hard on the mouth...

I jerked awake—shaking all over—disoriented and paralyzed with fear.
Even after I returned to the present, I couldn't sleep for hours.

PROLOGUE

"Mom, I want to talk to you—in your room," Susan stormed. She was nineteen. She rushed me to the bedroom and slammed the door.

"Do you know what's happened to Karla?" Karla was ten. I didn't know that anything had happened to her, but Susan didn't wait for an answer.

"She just told me that when she went fishing with Uncle Lee, he messed around with her. He made her fondle him. Mom—he was awful!"

"He did?" I heard myself say in a faint, far-away voice that made Susan even more irate.

"Mom, you have to DO something—NOW! What's the matter with you?"

"I don't know. I can't think..."

Susan gave up on me and flung herself out of the room. I sat there blinking like a toad, but I couldn't feel any anger, or find any words, or conceive any idea about what I should do. I was just numb. Lee is my brother. Something clicked inside when Susan told me—leaving me confused and incapacitated.

At the time it didn't register why I heard Susan's anger, but couldn't respond; why I suddenly became so helpless and unable to feel anything at all. Caught up in a pattern of numb helplessness, I couldn't associate my strange manner with its hidden cause. More than twenty years later after wrestling with the impacts and the discovery of more and more abuses spanning at least three generations, I finally made the connection. But it was on that day that Karla had exposed the first clue to our family's hidden legacy.

PART ONE

"You cannot know where you're going
until you know where you've come from."

James Farmer

1

THE HOMECOMING

I follow my memories back to a summer day in 1947, when I was twenty-seven.

Windows open, the gray-blue Chevy club coupe is heading north, nearing the end of our annual trek from Santa Barbara to the family ranch, sixty miles north of San Francisco. It's Karin's turn in the front seat. "Tempted and Tried," she begins to sing one of her favorites. Susan and I join in. Unmindful of the message, we know all the words and love to sing in the car—on our way to anywhere. We give it all we have.

"Tempted and tried, we're oft made to wonder,
Why it should be thus, all the day long;
Why there are others, living around us,
Never molested, though in the wrong.

"Farther along we'll know more about it,
Farther along we'll understand why.
Cheer up, my brother; live in the sunshine,
We'll understand it all by and by." *

Fair, wavy-haired Susan, age seven, and four-year-old Karin with her thick brown braids are barely able to contain their excitement. Bursting from the car, they rush into their grandparents' open arms, none the worse for their long day.

How unchanged my parents are since last year. They both look well and are quick to laugh, as the girls chatter on, while we go in the house. Dad's dark hair makes him look younger than his sixty-three years. Even though he's always been thin, his heavy cotton, tan-colored clothes enhance his healthy appearance. Mom's auburn hair has lightened a bit and she still keeps it carefully waved. Under her apron she's wearing a neat blue dress in the "Casual Country" mode. However, neither of them has ever taken country living casually. They both

*Traditional

1

work hard. They just know how to make the Ranch a place for others to enjoy. This convivial atmosphere is what clings to me when I'm away—almost crowding out the disturbing memories.

My younger brothers, Eric, Bob and Lee (all in their twenties), are gathering with other relatives for one of Mother's delicious Sunday dinners. At the end of the living room, a huge redwood slab supported by two small tables makes a handsome base for the ranch-grown food, served in colorful pottery. A bowl of bright zinnias completes it.

Conversation is cheerful during our leisurely meal. We have not been together for some time and enjoy talking over new plans or recent changes in our lives. Afterwards we carry our coffee outside to the terrace, which overlooks Sonoma Valley. We settle ourselves to watch the opposite hills turn purple in the late afternoon. Dad, restricted to a demi-tasse by his doctor, finishes his coffee, and rising says, "I need to move the garden hoses and check the pump. Come with me, Susan and Karin. There's a new swing down by the barn—waiting just for you."

Another surprise—he's so good to them.

Our tone and mood are light as we recall narrow escapes and surgeries we experienced when growing up. While others talk, my thoughts run—

...feels almost comfortable to be with my brothers now—still feel less mature than Eric, who is two years younger—and the older we get, the truer this seems—but I still feel like Bob's and Lee's older sister.

Meandering back to our childhood—

I remember when we were small—climbing a large tree in the back yard. Bob and Lee nearing the top— Eric and I halfway up, when Bob's branch broke. He bounced off branches all the way down, and I was so scared when he dropped by me. A big limb finally stopped him—knocked out his breath—and he couldn't cry. We got him safely to the ground—only scratched— not broken—and we were so relieved. I knew then that I didn't want anything bad to happen to my brothers, but I never could tell them how I felt. I can't tell them now either, even when we're being nice to each other.

Instead, I reminisce about Lee's visit to the hospital after my appendectomy. Chuckling, I say, "He popped under my bed, pretending to be the Troll in 'The Three Billy Goats Gruff,' and thundered,

'Who's going over my bridge?' I burst out laughing, felt stabbed, and grabbed my sore side. 'Please, Lee, stop being funny,' I begged. 'It hurts so much to laugh.'"

"Did I stop?" asks Lee, who has forgotten the incident.

"Oh, finally," I tease.

Warmed by the moment, I recall that Mother had the same surgery when she, too, was a teenager, but it didn't heal promptly as mine had.

"What was the most painful thing you can remember, Mom?" I ask, anticipating her funny remarks about her scar.

"Having YOU!" she snipes.

Stunned, not only by her answer, but by her vehemence, I pull inside myself and quietly shut down. Guilt enfolds me like a shroud. I watch shadows darken the gentle hills across the valley, knowing—

She'll never forgive me, because she doesn't love me
like Dad does. She never has.

Someone jumps into the loaded silence with another topic, but I feel derailed and cannot get back on track. It hurts too much. "I'm going to see how the girls are doing on the new swing," I mumble, as I head for the path to the barn.

The narrow path, formed years before by the Ranch goats, skirts the slope between the house and the barn and edges above Dad's terraced garden—tomatoes, eggplants, green peppers, yellow crook neck squashes and Kentucky Wonder beans on rows of tall poles.

I move quickly away from my debacle on the terrace, then slow down deliberately.

I need time alone.

Mother's words are pumping through me like poisoned darts and I can't turn back their pain, or pretend she didn't mean them. I remember the particulars I was told about my birth and sense for the first time the deep split that occurred between us when my body was torn from hers. I knew that the phases of the moon or Nature's own rhythm did not control the process. Her doctor did. I was born by appointment on July 16, 1920 in Illinois. As I continue down the path, I become once again the solemn six year-old listening to my mother:

"It was so simple to have the doctor plan which day it would be so that Dad and I wouldn't have to drive from Highland Park to Chicago after labor began. I checked into St. Luke's Hospital the afternoon before, then we went out to dinner with friends. It was fun. They took pictures of me in my big dress and made it a jolly celebration. Afterward

I had a good night's sleep in the hospital. The next morning the nurse gave me a shot and from then on it was dreadful!"

I hurt her—she didn't like me.

"The rules for babies were very strict. When I took you home, the doctor said I had to keep you on a four-hour feeding schedule, even if you cried in between. So I did. You cried a lot and I didn't dare pick you up. I didn't know anything about babies. I couldn't disobey the doctor."

I made her tired and unhappy.

"You were terribly active when you were little—always into things and you climbed everywhere. I had to watch you every minute. One time I came into the room just after you had escaped from your pen. You were up on the table where my favorite vase was. Before I could cross the room, you scrambled across the table and picked up the vase. 'Wait, Barbara, give it to me,' I said, but you looked me right in the eye and smashed it!"

"I'm sorry, Mommy, I wish I hadn't." I really wish you remembered the goods, not just the bads—I wonder: Why don't you like me?

As I near the barn, Dad hails me from the pump, and we follow the girls' voices to the swing. Before I join them, I tuck my child-me recollections back inside and put on the smile that covers over everything.

Both girls seem completely happy to be back on the Ranch. "Oh, Mommy, the swing's so big and goes so high," calls Karin, her hairbows bobbing as she throws her head back, and pumps her feet.

"Let's give Mommy a turn," says Susan, with a mischievous twinkle in her eye.

"Only if you promise to stop when I tell you," I plead, half-seriously.

"OK. Mom, I know you get dizzy on swings—but when you were little you loved them, didn't you?"

"Just as much as you and Karin do." And I wonder why aspects of my childhood keep recurring in family conversations. Even the girls are picking up on it.

Many years after that homecoming, I knew I had to retrieve those early memories once again, for a more careful look. I had to try to understand why I always felt so unsure of myself within the family.

2

FIRST CHILD

1920-1927

My birth had followed two miscarriages. Although I wasn't told that my being a girl was a disappointment, I don't remember ever hearing that my arrival was a joyous occasion. However, when my brother was born two years later, Dad was jubilant. He sent out telegrams saying, "Red-headed Eric has arrived," and the next day a follow-up, "My mistake—it ain't red." I translated his exuberance as an expression of relief. He had finally produced a son to carry on his name in a proud tradition that went back eight generations.

My father's career as a pipe salesman for construction projects was going well and they bought a large corner house in Geneva, a suburb of Chicago. After the twins Bob and Lee were born when I was five, a three-story wing was added. There was a nurse for the twins and a married couple "living in" took care of the home and cooking.

While they were babies, Mother was quite absorbed with the care of my brothers. When I was six, I remember walking to the doctor's office alone to receive a smallpox vaccination. I was afraid because I knew it would hurt, but I went.

During this period Dad became my primary parent. He took care of me when I was sick, and at night he carried me up to bed. We had a ritual that began with a bow to the clock and a solemn, "Good night, Mr. Clock." This was followed by his singing us up the stairs, "Climb, climb, climb the highest mountain—sailing up in a balloon. All amongst the little starlights—sailing 'round the silvery moon." I loved to have him put me to bed.

I could almost forget the shadowy feelings I also had when I was with him sometimes. I had them when we played our "ride the horsey" game. I would climb onto his foot, and while he held my hands, he moved his foot up and down in short, quick jerks, saying,

"The little girl goes to town trot, trot, trot, trot," and—
I smile in anticipation.

5

Next a higher, smoother gait—

"The little boy goes to town tee-canter, tee-canter, tee-canter, tee-canter,"

I giggle and feel "prickly" between my legs.

Now his foot moves abruptly from side to side—

"The old lady goes to town pace, pace, pace, pace,"

Nearly falling off, I'm laughing—but feeling tickled and *frightened—not afraid he'll drop me—afraid of what's happening down inside me.*

Finally, he catches me under my arms, and throws his leg as high as he can—

"And the old man—HE goes to town TEE-gallop, TEE-gallop, TEE-gallop, TEE-gallop."

I'm shouting gleefully and can't stop.

But I clearly remember the double aspects to my excitement. I anticipated the thrill of being tossed in the air, while confusing and scary sexual sensations hit me. I can see his wanton expression and recall my uncontrollable laughter as he pulled me back and forth on his foot.

Baby me at play, with Dad.

As far back as I can remember I received mixed sexual messages from my parents. Dad found sex funny and teased Mother by telling her off-color jokes. Although I didn't understand them at the time, I remembered his words and understood them later.

In contrast, Mother's attitude toward sex was certainly not playful. She presumed that my playmates and I were unusually curious about our bodies when we were out playing, so she frequently badgered me with questions. She used the guestroom for these little seminars and I dreaded the routine of going into this neat, seldom-used room.

She would shut the door as we entered and then motion to me to sit down.

I try not to squirm as she looks searchingly into my eyes. My stomach becomes a tight knot. I'm scared, even though I haven't been bad.

"I called you in because you were playing behind the bushes and I couldn't see you. What were you doing?"

"The bushes are our fort. We were hiding from the others."

"Is that *all* you were doing?"

"Yes."

"I am afraid that you sometimes hide from me in there." She's staring into my eyes and I try to keep from blinking.

"You know you must not take off your clothes to look at each other because it's wrong to giggle and be silly about your bodies."

"Mommy, we weren't doing that. We were just playing." She ignores me.

"When the boys saw you, how much did you show them? Did you touch the boys?"

"Oh no, we just looked—but, Mommy, we don't do that anymore."

Her questions are so scary—why does she think we would be so bad?

She always ends these sessions with, "When you're married you will want to have intercourse with your husband and it will be a beautiful experience. You know that's how babies begin."

I never could make the connection from the non-touching rule we observed in the bushes to an unimaginable participation in the bridal bed. And I increasingly felt attacked by her interrogations.

I often felt isolated and alone in my family during these years. Although I enjoyed playing with both boys and girls in our neighborhood, I didn't like being the only girl at home and frequently played by myself in my room.

I didn't like dolls, because I couldn't imagine their responses and didn't care to "mother" them by dressing and pretending to feed them. My favorite companion at home was invisible Barbara (who shared my name and my life). I developed private games with her, using my carpet like a huge gameboard. It was light gray—plain in the center, with a wide border on all four sides, full of designs in various darker tones. On each corner of the carpet was a large rosette, plus two more in the middle of each border.

Barbara and I played by the hour on that border, going from one rosette to the next. We didn't have dice to tell us how far to go at a time—we just discussed it and knew. I loved playing both roles and feeling as though I was in charge of both of us.

Dad was often full of new ideas, some of them artistic, others wholesome and fun. He and I made a miniature Japanese garden together and I felt very close to him as we worked on it. We painted the tiny figures ourselves and arranged the plants in a large round dish. We put a delicate pagoda on a mound, with a curving path of pebbles leading up. There was moss beside the path and dwarf ivy spilled over the edge of the dish. An arched bridge across a stone stream, and our little people on the path, completed this Japanese fairyland. It was like pictures in my favorite *Book House* book and I pretended the people were alive. I loved it. Later I was given a Japanese puzzle box that reminded me of this garden. It became my most prized possession.

When I was six and before I had learned how to swim, Mother and a friend took me to a public swimming pool. They were not dressed for swimming and sat in chairs beside the pool. It was a woodsy setting and the pool had a sloping, mossy bottom.

When I started slipping beyond my depth, I couldn't stop. I called to Mother, who was chatting with her friend and wasn't watching me. She didn't hear me. I kept sliding farther away from the edge, into the deeper water, while splashing and kicking as hard as I could. Nothing worked. I began—

> *Screaming to Mother—last breath—gulping in water—choking—chest splitting. Terrified—thrashing—going down.*

Just as I went completely under, I caught a glimpse of a red bathing suit, diving in from the bank. Then everything faded away. Moments later, he pulled me to the surface and brought me in. Someone revived me. But I never knew who the boy in the red suit was. He saved my life.

After that I did learn to swim. Eventually I dared to jump from high boards, but my respect for the water is tremendous. The memory of helplessly sliding under stays with me and will always be associated with Mother's lack of concern for my safety. Afterward when she wrapped me up in my towel, I sensed her fear, but her touch did not comfort me.

Mother became the leader of my Brownie troop and was called the Brown Owl. We all had brown uniforms and she had a pretty Brown Owl pin on hers. On Tuesdays we wore our uniforms to school and I felt special all day. After school the others came home with me.

"Twit twoo, twit twoo," calls Brown Owl, and we hurry into the living room/woodland. "Hello Brownies, are you all ready for the meeting?"

"Yes, Brown Owl, we're ready."

Mommy is a friendly, happy Brown Owl and I'm never scared of her at our meetings.

Today she has a surprise activity for us. "We're going to find a pool in the forest and make pictures of the little creatures that live there."

"You mean like frogs and fishes?" someone asks.

"Can there be gnomes and fairies, too?" asks another.

"They can be anything you believe lives there," answers Brown Owl, and off we go to find the forest pool.

"We must be very quiet, or we'll scare them away," she cautions, as we tiptoe quietly around the room and down the rug-strip/trail. There behind the chair/tree we find the large-round-plateglass-over-dark-blue-fabric/pool with real leaves all around it. We form a circle and take turns asking our forest friends to join us. Then we sit around a table, drawing our pool creatures.

After juice and cookies our meeting closes with all of us saying "Good-bye" to Brown Owl. I say it, too, and go out with the others, pretending we're leaving our forest.

The meetings were fun because Mother could drop her worries about me temporarily, when she was using her talents with this group of little girls. I was just one of the others and we were at ease together.

3

HOW IT BEGAN

In our neighborhood boys and girls played together, enjoying activities preferred by boys: building forts, making sandpile roads for Tinkertoy cars, and lots of play on swings, slides and trapezes. I loved being included with boys my own age whom I also knew at school.

Since I often felt scared when I was alone and apprehensive when I was with the family, I began to wish I, too, was a boy. They always seemed happier and stronger than I. Sometimes I privately pretended I was a boy.

When Dad started taking the family to secluded spots in the woods or countryside, the boy-wish became much stronger. One of these places was near a lake. Oak and evergreen trees provided some shade, but I remember how the hot sun hit us when we got out of the car. My brothers and I wanted to take off our sandals and play at the edge of the water.

Instead we followed Dad on a path to a high board fence where he told us to take off all our clothes, so we could go swimming. We didn't bring our swimsuits and I wanted Mother to say no, but she never did, although she didn't seem to share Dad's enthusiasm. Sideways, I watched her undress—embarrassed for both of us.

I can see Dad now, running naked into the cold water and turning quickly around with a loud whoop. He joked to my brothers about the shock coming to their genitals, as he urged us all to join him. The boys seemed to be having fun. They romped around, in and out of the water, squealed and laughed. I pretended, but I couldn't enjoy it. I also couldn't reveal any hesitancy or displeasure. Our parents were trying to throw off their Victorian upbringing, and I knew that any doubts of mine would have been ridiculed.

I was receiving another sex lesson; namely, my feelings about displaying my body were different from the rest of the family, therefore unacceptable. The best thing to do was to pretend my feelings didn't exist. It didn't feel good to be me.

When we were undressed, I felt exposed and uneasy. I hated my body and wished I could disappear. From then on, I never felt safe or that I had any rights to privacy. Dad not only knew I was embarrassed—he delighted in it. I believed he knew something about our bodies that we didn't. His way of watching us made his eyes glitter, and he always laughed in a knowing manner. At those times he was someone else—not my companionable father, with whom I felt close. He seemed to exude a tremendous power that made me feel helpless. I felt very lonely when we were naked.

It's not that I wasn't curious about sexuality, because I was. As children sometimes do, my friends and I looked at each other now and then. But among peers, it was an entirely different experience than being nude with my family. We all assumed we were being naughty, and that we'd be lectured if caught. This was accepted, and we did it anyway.

But when with the family I envied my brothers because they had each other. I wished my body was like theirs, especially when we were all naked; I wanted to feel I was one of them. They were obviously pleased to be boys. I dreaded the prospect of looking like Mother some day, with large breasts hanging down.

When Mother talked to me in the guest room, she never mentioned masturbation, but I hated to touch myself, even accidentally. It wasn't a question of being good or bad. It was the frightening awareness of something happening within me that I didn't understand and couldn't control. When it occurred, I felt as vulnerable to the caprices of my body as I was to the caprices of my dad, and I feared them both.

Although I can't remember what he did to me when I was very little, I do recall that I was deeply afraid of him when he was naked—even when we were with the family. I remember that I became phobically aware of my genitals, wished I could put my panties back on, and always felt vulnerable when there was no cloth covering them. I was terrified of being hurt there and anxious about their mysterious sensations. My body seemed to be sending me messages of warning, in a foreign language that I couldn't understand.

When I shoved these feelings down, others came up to take their place—troubling, angry feelings directed at those who weren't intimidating like my dad. Sudden rage would grip me while I was playing and I would explode at a friend—cursing obscenities at the top of my lungs. While these eruptions were disguising their source, my buried fears spawned other behavior that was not normal; behavior that shouldn't have occurred to a seven-year-old girl. One incident, in particular, speaks to what was happening to me.

We had a young Sealyham dog that my uncle had given us, who quickly became part of the family. We all loved Pat and he seemed fond of each of us, without a favorite.

One day I carried him up to my room, locked the door, and laid him on his side on the gray carpet. I then began to masturbate him. Although I had seen dogs mate, I didn't associate this with mating. I knew what to do with my fingers to make him climax. He didn't resist and I knew that he enjoyed it. I remember thinking that I didn't want anyone to know what I was doing, but that he liked it, so it must be a little bit okay. I knew that pretty soon "gooey stuff" would come out and that it wouldn't be urine. When it did, I was satisfied that everything happened the way I expected it to.

After the "research" was over that day, I had no desire to repeat it. I knew that Mother would be horrified if she knew about it, and I suddenly felt guilty and deeply ashamed of what I had done. But I felt safe because Pat couldn't tell on me. Whenever I remembered the incident, though, I felt like a dirty, bad girl and hated myself.

Before this I had been enjoying the privacy of my room with invisible Barbara, my constant companion for more than four years. When my parents scolded me, I calmly blamed her for my misdeeds, although I no longer did so out loud as I had when I was very small. But this lapse of hers into sexual misbehavior had changed our relationship. She had become much too naughty for me to trust. So I did the only thing I could think of to get her (and the badness) out of my life. I put her down on one of the rosettes in my carpet. Then I stamped and stamped on her, sobbing, "You're dead, you're dead—now you're dead!"

I was all alone. I had destroyed the friend who had always accepted my blame and made me feel better. I no longer believed in her magical ability to alleviate my guilt. Now there was no one to blame but myself. From then on guilt settled around and within me like a heavy, noxious gas. I couldn't outgrow it, for it expanded along with me. It was always there.

By the time I was in third grade Mother had become convinced that the neighborhood children's interest in sex was abnormal and bound to lead me into serious trouble. She was frightened. In addition, unsettling suspicions about Dad's sexual preoccupations were surely creeping into her consciousness by then. When she heard about a fine private school in another town, we left the large home and moved into a small bungalow on the outskirts of Downers Grove. I was nine and entering the fourth grade.

1929

In our new house the boys shared a large playroom upstairs, over the kitchen. My bedroom was downstairs, across the hall from my parents' room.

One night Mother was out of town. After my brothers were asleep, Dad suggested that I sleep in Mother's bed—as a special treat—and I was pleased. I wasn't afraid because I thought we had left all the scary badness behind in our old house. So far, the move had given us children new things to think about, and we were enjoying ourselves.

That night I had wiggled myself into a sleeping position on my stomach and closed my eyes, when Dad came into the darkened room. He spoke my name softly and did not turn on the light. When he sat down on the edge of the bed, I was surprised.

"Shhhhh," he said, as he gently turned me over and carefully unbottoned my one-piece pajamas. I froze. He lifted my arms to remove the top part, then pulled them off over my feet. He slid into bed beside me. He was naked.

"I want to teach you about your body so that you will be a good wife someday."

Buzzing, buzzing in my head—sinking, sinking—

He stroked, petted, and kissed me all over, while he whispered, snuggled, and caressed me. Although he didn't physically hurt me, I felt frantic and helpless—like when I was drowning. I could hardly breathe.

Numbness floated me away from feeling his body, his hands, his lips, his fingers. I turned into a Raggedy Ann doll. I couldn't speak or move. I pretended he was caressing someone else and I was just watching; but I knew it was me inside the Raggedy Ann doll.

He said, "This is our own, special secret and we won't tell anyone."

Oh Daddy, this is too scary! Who are we? What is happening?

But I couldn't ask him out loud. He had become a stranger I didn't know and didn't want to know. My world had crumbled away.

Afterward I couldn't think of him as being all bad, because he wasn't. I remembered the good times and helpful lessons that he taught me—memories which distorted reality and fed my confusion. When his old self returned, periodically, flashes of my devotion rushed in to chase away the nightmare. One time several months later, I clearly recall feeling close to him again. It was like a sudden summer shower—unexpected, warm and pleasant. But it happened in the winter. I was chosen to lead the carollers in our Christmas play at school and we trooped onto the stage singing, "Here We Come A'Wassailing." Then I sang, "The First Noel" as a solo. It surprised my parents. Later, as we crunched through the snow to our car, Dad said, "When I heard you sing all by yourself, it brought a big lump to my throat." I glowed inside at his praise. My real father was back.

I tried not to think about our secret, but when he reminded me, "Always keep it—never tell," I couldn't forget it. I didn't blame him, because I truly believed that my daddy wouldn't do anything wrong. And I trusted him to take care of me. But I hated his latest "lesson" and sensed he wasn't finished.

THE ESSENCE

One recent morning while running, I was unexpectedly reminded of that aspect of my childhood that made me feel trapped in harmful, unhealthy circumstances I couldn't change or avoid.

I had been jogging briskly along, enjoying an early morning's crisp, sunny air—with the quiet interrupted now and then by the cries of gulls over the nearby river—when along came a huge truck. I stopped a moment at the edge of the road. After it passed, I continued on.

I became immediately aware of the sickening smell of the truck's exhaust—even though it was invisible. I realized my heart and lungs, accelerated by exercise, were pumping those carbon monoxide-loaded fumes into my system. It was too late to slow down the intake process by walking; and it was impossible to avoid breathing long enough to get beyond the polluted area.

The inevitability of harm struck me as being similar to the invasive damage of sexual assaults on a child. The emotional essence of incest is to feel oneself becoming spoiled to the core and powerless to stop it.

4

CHILDHOOD UNDER SIEGE

1929-1931

The more I remember how I behaved as a child, the more I remember how I felt. Throughout childhood my wish to be a boy continued. Boys had more fun than girls; when my brothers played together I envied them their easy companionship. Later on, as Dad's sexual assaults continued, my boy-wish spiraled into enormous frustration and anger. Because I couldn't be one, there were times when I hated boys. Feeding these emotions was my firm conviction that I was less loved than my brothers.

My feelings for them were always confused and often conflicting. When we were playing amiably together, I liked them. I even tried to look out for them, as when Bobby fell from the top of the tree. But I was also easily enraged and quickly switched to mistreating them. Aside from teasing me, I don't recall that they ever did anything serious enough to incite my violent responses. I only remember some of the ways I tried to hurt them.

One afternoon I pushed all three down the basement stairs. They did a lot of yelling, but were not seriously hurt. Later Dad came home and spanked me and I loathed my brothers for making such a fuss about it. When a friend of Mother's said to me one day, "How lucky you are to have three brothers. Do you have a favorite?" I glumly responded, "No, I hate them all the same!"

My main outlet for these overwhelming feelings of alienation became an intense urge to fight the world—or at least my corner of it—which meant my brothers and many of the boys at school. On the slightest provocation, I fought hard, and to win, and usually did. I wanted to prove what I often bragged—that I could "beat up" every boy I knew.

Beneath it all, I felt hurt and scared most of the time. I desperately wanted my dad to stop molesting me. But where he was concerned, I was powerless. So I took it out on my brothers and the other boys.

This quick temper led me into one battle after another. I don't remember feeling any pain when I was hit; I just remember punching the boys as hard as I could. And I fought with my fists like a boy—never kicking or crying like a girl. I tried to be tough, no matter what it cost in terms of pain or punishment. At school this meant they immediately separated me from the others, but I never received any form of abuse by the teachers.

That wasn't the case at home. Dad's hard spankings were extremely painful and left me feeling totally beaten. Another punishment we dreaded was having our legs switched by Mother. We had to cut our own switches. The thinner and longer they were, the more they stung, so we were careful to have them sufficiently pain-inducing for her to accept. If they weren't, she would cut them herself. We walked a narrow line in our approach to switch-cutting.

Before and after that time in Mother's bed, my memory for specifics is blurred. Trying to recall details, (where-when-what) is like driving my car during a heavy downpour at night, without windshield wipers. There are bits and pieces which I know are parts of it, between spaces where my memory turned itself off years ago.

I never wanted anything he did, but I knew I couldn't dissuade him; so whenever we were alone I slipped "away" into a trancelike state. Then, not knowing if he was going to molest me wasn't so scary. But I knew I was trapped. Even the trances couldn't allay my growing sense of disgrace, deception, and despair.

I have no memory of arousal during Dad's humiliating "lessons." I just remember going numb and feeling paralyzed—unable to move—when he began to touch me. Each time it was frightening, like being tumbled by a giant wave—hoping I could hold my breath until I was able to surface. And his assaults were not limited to using his fingers. I wish I could forget his naked body arched over me while he explored my genitals with his tongue.

To the child-me, yesterday is still today...
Dad and Eric and I are taking the overnight train up to Wisconsin, where Mother will meet us in the car with the twins. Then we'll drive up to a summer cabin on Ephraim Bay.

Clickety clack—clickety clack—*It's a long car with many passengers, and everyone is visiting, reading, or looking out the windows. Evening—trees and houses rush by, with lights coming on here and there.*

The porter comes and prepares our berths. He puts up a ladder to the top one.

"Daddy, can I sleep up there?"

"Sure you can. Eric and I will sleep in the lower one."

Then the porter snaps down the window shades and puts up the heavy, dark green curtains on the aisle. Like magic, each berth becomes a private room.

With a goodnight kiss from Dad, I climb up to my berth and he hands me my pajamas. I start to undress. The train lurches around turns—Funny to unbutton, untie, and pull clothes off over my head with the train moving so fast—Funny to pull on my pajamas sitting down. Finally I'm sliding in between smooth sheets with a woolly blanket on top. There are large dark letters on it—CHICAGO AND NORTHWESTERN.

Clickety clack—clickety clack—*Feels good lying here in my little room, with the rocking motion and the even sound—like a lullaby. The car is very quiet—just the rhythmic rolling of the wheels on the tracks beneath all of us. I love this train. I love this trip. I loved eating supper in the dining car. I even love Eric, we're having such a good time.*

Eyes closing—clickety clacks softer—drifting off—

New sound—eyes flash open—heart pounding.

Curtain moving—ladder thuds on its bar.

"Oh no, oh no," inside myself.

Quick whispered, "Shhhh." He's climbing in.

He's turning back the sheet and blanket—removing my pajamas.

Raggedy Ann doll—can't speak or move. Hours of numbness.

Train moving through the long night.

Below Eric sleeps on alone.

Much as I dreaded his intrusions, I believed Dad when he said he was teaching me how to make love, to prepare me for marriage. "I want you to enjoy being with your husband and doing what couples are supposed to do. After you children were born, your mother hasn't wanted to very often. I don't want you to grow up that way." Since they had all the children they said they wanted, Mother's lack of interest didn't seem unreasonable to me. But I had no cause to doubt his motivation. I had never heard of a father sexually abusing his child.

Both my parents seemed anxious about my sexuality. Because they frequently expressed their concerns (although in opposite ways), I soon believed that there was something seriously wrong with me. They treated me as if I were flawed in some mysterious way and I accepted their opinions without question. Their talk and actions made me feel thoroughly unclean. Although I hated being alone with either one of them, I assumed that they were trying to set me straight.

Dad always cautioned me not to tell anyone about what he was doing to me. Later he said, "When you are grown-up and married, you can tell your husband about it." My inner voice asked—

Why should I do that? Ohhh, I don't want to ever get
married.I don't want to be a wife!

"But you must never tell anyone else," he went on. "It will always be a private matter between the three of us."

Now I know he wanted to be sure I wouldn't tell Mother. But he needn't have worried because I tried to avoid personal talks with her. Furthermore, I couldn't conceive of his doing anything wrong—ever. I thought that as a participant in something that felt wrong, even though I was unwilling—*I* was the one who was bad. The possibility it was *his* "badness" didn't occur to me. His behavior was incomprehensible, so I soon drifted away from reality, assuming his guilt as my own.

It was confusing to have him woo me sexually, treat me as a confidante about Mother, and then be very intolerant of me if I disagreed with her. If she was upset, I was punished. Publicly he expected me to respect her, while his private behavior destroyed that possibility. He made our lives a lie.

As their child, I craved their approval and love, but it seemed beyond my reach. Mother's attitude was predictable. I thought she usually worried about me, didn't like me very much, and wished that I was different. But I never knew how I stood with Dad from one day to the next. Sometimes he was the warm, fun-loving father I had when I was little; at other times he seemed a harsh, cold stranger who hated the sight of me. In between I was his child-wife.

Dad was often cunning when I least expected it, casting sly innuendoes that made me want to run away.

I'm wheeling my bike from the garage, preparing to join my friends. Suddenly he appears by the bushes on the other side of the driveway. Since he is standing in the path, I feel ambushed and can't avoid him, but seeing the familiar glitter in his eyes, I want to. He stops me—his hand on the handlebar.

Leering at my crotch, he asks, "Does your bicycle seat tickle you 'down there' and make you feel good when you're riding?" I am almost ten and trying to create a clean, guilt-free life for myself. Bike-riding is a joy— a release from my family. I hate his idea that it's a form of masturbation. But I can't let him see my true feelings. I try to look blank as I mumble an embarrassed, "No."

He seemed compelled to startle, embarrass, and arouse us all in one way or another, often through rough-housing—his pajamas gaping open—while covertly tickling our genitals. I believe it affected each of us in a variety of ways—none of them healthy. For me, the distortion of my sensual responses, and his obsession with them, triggered a preoccupation that disturbed me. I began to develop a distracting concern about how we are supposed to function sexually.

To consult my parents for answers was unthinkable. And our gang was a collection of girls and boys, among whom gender was unimportant. We were active, loyal, and imaginative in our play; but not interested in seeing each other undressed, or in discussing sex. Since there was no one I could trust with my questions, I tried to ignore them. But they wouldn't go away.

While those were wholesome years with my friends, they were increasingly confusing at home. My relationship with Mother was focused on not arousing her concern. In an ironic contrast, I frequently felt less bothered by Dad.

When he was away, my thoughts about him often joined those about my life at school. I found I had so much to tell him. And I assumed that he was as interested in knowing as I was in sharing.

While he was spending a winter in Pittsburg due to his work, I missed him and pretended our awful secret wasn't real. I often wrote to "Dearst old Dad," and once I asked him to explain his iron pipe business that was keeping him away for so long.

I always quickly sealed up the letters, so that Mother couldn't read them first. She said she just wanted to check the spelling, but I knew it was more than that. My letters were just for him.

Febuary 5, 1931
<u>Thursday</u>

BARBARA CLAIRE SMALL
1600 GEORGE STREET
DOWNER'S GROVE, ILL.

Dearst old Dad;
        I got your letter
to-night. And I was glad to
hear all about your pipe. It
got me less mixed up.
        In school we are going to
stop studying the Egyptains
and start studying The Greeks,
then we are going to study the
Romans, then the Chinest.
But before we leave the
Egyptains I am going to
tell you an Egyptains
poem.   [Turn over]

I learned this in school.

An Egyptain Poem

I am the pure Lotus,
Spring ing up in Splendor
Fed by the breath of Ra.

Rising into sunlight
Out of soil and darkness,
I blossom in the field,

~~~~ Amond and Ra were
two
the sun gods. But after while
they made ~~them~~ into one god
and called them Amond Ra.

wrote when Through Reading Poem

I will send this letter when I send the book which will be soon

Love
Bubs

A kiss for all you hard work

P.S.
If not to much bother will you please print it's hard to read when you write fast.

This is an example of my feelings for him, despite what he did. I now call it "negative or destructive bonding."

Now it's summer and he's home. Today we are alone in the car, singing some funny old songs. I'm so happy to be with him again. He begins a new one, calling it a fraternity song, but I don't know what it means. Before beginning another, he instructs me, "Some day when college boys start singing these songs, you should say you've already heard them all."

I am beginning to feel uneasy.

He sings one about "young bulls with their long, red bars," which I don't understand. I don't like it. When I sit there silently beside him, looking straight ahead at the road, he glances over at me, laughs, and sings it again.

> *I'm afraid of him now—there's a knot in my stomach—and I'm almost crying. I wish he really was my Dearst old Dad. I want to go home and be alone in my room.*

I had often watched animals mate, and was puzzled when a neighbor's dog would try to "mate" my leg. One afternoon I got down on all fours to see if he would try to mate with me. I was completely covered with heavy clothes, and intrigued by his futile attempts. The incident ended when I looked up to see my mother and brothers watching through the window. That time Mother was speechless. There wasn't any lecture.

It's strange that I made no attempt to find a concealed location for this experiment. I was in the open yard in broad daylight. Did I unconsciously seek punishment to relieve my chronic sense of shame? For years I wondered why, when I was so passive during the ordeals with Dad, I would go to the opposite extreme and allow the dog to become so excited.

I had never heard of animal-human activities and I'm certain the idea was prompted by the dog's sexual aggressiveness; but my response to him was different from everyone else's. They just pushed him away. Was I acting out an unconscious cry for aid—as though I were shouting, "Something is not right in my life—Help!"?

I began to feel that I was two different persons. At school, I was an eager participant in all the activities with teachers and friends. Even though they had seen my temper flareups, they didn't know my sinful other person even existed. At home this "other" felt constantly on the brink of disaster. Our maid was the only one I could trust to be in my corner, no matter what I did. Were my brothers going to provoke me?

Was I going to be punished? Would my parents ever love me? **What was the matter with me?**

Although I was permitted to be a tomboy, Mother frequently reminded me not to be selfish, not to get angry, and never to lose my temper. I saw my father lose his temper often (apparently acceptable for males), but Mother was always extremely fearful about my anger and loss of control, so I became a mountain of repressed rage that periodically erupted. I felt I was a freaky misfit, incapable of proper conduct—doomed to live down to Mother's low opinion of me.

Part of the reality of my childhood were the positive experiences, woven in between the others, which provided cherished memories of normalcy. My first awareness of a sensitive self hiding within came through my responses to music. We didn't have a piano. Instead I had a cardboard keyboard and taught myself to read the notes. I hummed the simple tunes and "played" them on the "keys."

After my lessons began, I practiced early every morning on the school piano. By spring I was looking forward to my first recital, feeling prepared and eager to play. When my turn came I wasn't afraid and didn't even feel nervous when I struck a wrong note. I just apologized to the audience—then calmly started over. The piece was a favorite of beginning students, "The Happy Farmer." I wanted to play it perfectly, all the way through and with flourish. So I did.

The following year, in addition to a weekly lesson, I was invited to my teacher's home on Saturdays. Up early, I'd quickly clean my room, then speed over on my bike, music in the basket. She had two beautiful "baby grands"—we played duets for hours.

Finally we had an upright piano in our dining room. I was delighted and played almost constantly. The instrument was like a magnet and I couldn't resist its pull. Sometimes the family teased me about my "rubber arm", which could mysteriously reach the piano when they thought I was upstairs or out of the house. It was good-natured teasing. No one ever criticized me when I practiced. Whenever I played, I didn't worry about making mistakes. I just enjoyed it. At thirteen I gave my own recital one Sunday afternoon.

One of my happiest summers was spent in the country. We rented a farmhouse that was surrounded by pastureland, lovely rolling woods, and other farms. There was a big barn and joy of joys, I had a horse of my own for the whole summer. Every day I joined other girls my age from nearby farms and we rode our horses together through the fields and woods. Sometimes we went into town to pick up the mail. It was wonderful to be trusted with the care of this beloved creature, and to go off riding with my friends—free!

While I still fought with my brothers, I felt more secure at school and less hostile toward my schoolmates. My girl friends and I loved playing with the boys. We played soccer and softball, rode bikes with no hands, and sledded fast down snowy hills. In buckled galoshes with loop skis, I loved skiing down slopes with trees tricky to avoid. We played hockey in shorts, and went down the toboggan slide standing up, hanging onto the rope.

I rode horses bareback, and dreamed of going out West disguised as a cowboy. If I couldn't be a boy, I wanted to be thought of as one; be their chum and liked for the fun we shared on an equal basis. But I gradually became aware of an inner conflict. On the one hand, I wanted to be a pal, with no acknowledgment of our physical differences; and on the other, I was strongly attracted by these differences.

Finally, I wanted to know that I was admired by a boy. If I couldn't BE one, I wanted to HAVE one. David was my favorite. He was as well-mannered and self-controlled as I was temperamental. He also had a delightful sense of humor and we had good talks together. His enjoyment of my company was a comfort and a relief, for it helped me feel better about myself. I always remember him as a gentle-humored friend of the clean, untouched me I was trying to salvage.

David and the others in our gang provided a support they didn't know I needed. But they were only with me during the day. The long nights held a private terror for that solitary other-me.

5

LOSSES

Fall 1931

One day as I approached my bedroom, I heard a slight sound, peeked through a crack in the door, and discovered my father—his hands working with something on top of the bureau. I watched in horror, too stunned and afraid of his anger to move. He was breaking my Japanese puzzle box! It had always been special to me and in some symbolic way I identified with it. Its secret compartment gave me a wonderful feeling of having one safe, private place of my own.

Because I couldn't keep my brothers out of my room, I didn't display it and had it hidden in the back of my top drawer. But Dad had found it. Piece by carved piece, he tore it apart with his bare hands until it was just a pile of wooden scraps that could never be mended and whole again.

I slipped into the bathroom down the hall before he saw me, and waited there—hardly breathing—tears flowing. After he tramped by the bathroom door and down the stairs, I rushed to my room and gathered up the broken pieces. Then I quickly wrapped them in a scarf and tucked them in the back of my bottom drawer, underneath my sweater. I couldn't throw them away.

Afterward I never mentioned what I'd seen, but watching him destroy the box was like watching him destroy me, and I was gripped by sudden fear of him. I couldn't imagine why he would do such a thing, unless he hated me very much and wanted to hurt me deeply. He succeeded.

If I had not seen him doing it, I would have believed it was one of my brother's pranks; and my reaction would have been immediate and loud. It puzzles me that he left the pieces there for my predictable explosion and accusations. What was going through his mind when I behaved afterward as though nothing had happened? I never understood why he treated me as he did—his extremes of moods, anger, and fondling always baffled me. But it never occurred to me to question him. I always assumed that I was the one who was continually out of step with everyone else.

One morning while I was playing outside, I found myself getting too warm. So I took off my sweater. Then I went in the house, intending to go upstairs and put it away, but paused in the front hall when I heard Mother's voice. It was coming from the living room.

"....worried about Barbara, and I don't know what to do."

On hearing my name I had to listen for more, and tiptoed down the hall. Just before the archway leading into the living room I stopped and stood beneath the wall telephone in the corner.

"He said it would be good for her," Mother continued telling her friend. My heart began pounding.

"He said it would keep her from being nervous like me when we are in bed."

Oh Daddy, I thought it was our secret! Why did you break it?

"When I asked if she wasn't too young to understand about foreplay," Mother went on, "He said it was better to show her before she began to grow up; so she wouldn't get romantic about him."

What is she talking about!? Ohhh—Why did he tell her? And why is she telling her friend? Please, dear God, let me die. I don't want them to see me, ever again.

I pressed my face into the corner. My face, my face—that naked part of me I couldn't ever hide.

"Barbara has always been so difficult, as you know, so hard to handle," her voice continued. "I hoped she'd be happy in the new school. But she's worse than ever."

Oh, Mommy, you're never going to like me now.
I didn't want him to do it. I knew it was bad.

Mother, pressing her friend, asked, "What do you think? I really don't know what to do about her anymore."

"Well, I think it's very wrong," her friend responded, "but I know it would be hard for you to convince him and make him change."

Mother agreed, saying, "He knows I'm upset, but he's always said I'm too serious and idealistic about sex. So I'm not sure what he'll do."

Suddenly it's like being in a falling dream. Noise is in my head. Then I begin to shake all over. It stops the falling feeling, but I know now that there will be no stopping Dad.

I crept up to my room, closed the door, dropped the sweater on the chair, and found my bed. I pulled the blanket up over my head. Curled into a ball, I felt that I had been stripped in public and made permanently bare. I couldn't stop crying. Afterwards, remembering Mother's voice, especially when Dad was touching me, I felt like the guilty "other woman." But I was only her little girl.

When I recall Mother's accumulation of close friends, I find myself wondering if there were others in whom she confided about me and Dad. I'm thankful this didn't occur to me then, because I can't imagine coping with the thought that other women, sympathetic to Mother, knew about my "sinfulness." I never felt more defenseless and alone.

Although I had always had a room of my own, the doors seldom had locks and I never felt safe. My brothers would enter without knocking. If I were undressing and protested, they would tease me. Even Mother entered whenever she chose, ostensibly to tell me something that couldn't wait, while her eyes were checking out my body.

When I began maturing physically, I was upset about these changes, for they meant that I was less like the boy that I still would have preferred to be. Since intrusions by the family continued, my embarrassment heightened; I felt isolated, and at the same time beleaguered.

One of the most painful memories I have of the changes occurring during puberty was the derision of my brothers. The primary focus of their mirth was my "big seat." Since I couldn't see that part of my anatomy as directly as they, I knew I must have an ugly body.

If I sought relief from their taunts, Dad laughed and said, "You're finally getting what you deserve for being so mean to them." Because they were still young and impressionable, this encouragement of their ridicule was as unhealthy for their attitudes about females as it was painful for me to endure. We became thoroughly alienated. When Dad joined them and smirked at their jibes, I firmly believed that I really was a misshapen freak. Years later I saw a snapshot of myself as a twelve-year-old in a bathing suit and finally discovered that I had had a perfectly normal form. But at the time I believed them and felt sad that I bore no resemblance to my pretty best friend Alice—my chum since we were nine.

In addition to her appearance, I also admired Alice's cheery, untroubled manner. When we played at her home I felt no tension there, and since all my family was better behaved when we had a guest, I loved having her over. Later she vacationed with us, sometimes far from her home. Still good friends, she has recently told me she never suspected my shocking secret—further proof of how well it was hidden.

Polly was our housekeeper and my personal ally. She was always on my side and I knew it, even though she didn't say anything to countermand my parents. Sometimes during a fracas with my brothers, while Mother was scolding me, she managed to look me in the eye and let me feel her support. I knew I could trust her. She would never let me down or betray me in any way.

When she took me home with her on weekends now and then, she gave me a break from the on-going struggle of being with the family. We didn't discuss my situation; she just gave me happy times with her friends—one of whom was my age.

One afternoon when Mother was out, I came home late from school and gave Polly an elaborate excuse, saying I had been temporarily kidnapped, but had cleverly escaped. She gave me the same amused smile she gave me when I retaliated against my brothers' teasing—a smile which said she didn't believe me about the kidnapping, or blame me for being annoyed with my brothers.

It was a comfort to know exactly where I stood with her; to know she cared about me, was too intelligent to believe my phoney excuses, and was amused—not upset—by my trying to fool her. Despite my trust in her, though, I never considered confiding about my father. I couldn't risk losing her support by letting her know the terrible truth about myself. She didn't need to be told that something was wrong in order to communicate her awareness of my unfavored position in the family.

By this time my parents' friends often asked me to babysit with their children. Sometimes one of the mothers called me over when I was out playing, saying she needed to "get away" for awhile. I enjoyed feeding and caring for these toddlers. To me it was a job and I did my best, but I was never paid.

My friend Alice was paid for her services and I felt as deserving as she; so when adults took advantage of my abilities, I felt ashamed—less grown-up than Alice. Polly said that it was wrong of those parents not to pay me, but I was afraid of ridicule or criticism if I asked for payment. I felt indebted to most adults, but I never knew why.

One of Mother's most appealing qualities was her sense of fun and enjoyment of the ridiculous. On April Fool's Day she was especially creative in playing harmless pranks on all of us. The April Fool's Day when I was eleven began in the usual light-hearted way. Then my parents took my brothers into Chicago for the day while I remained at home with Polly.

Soon after they'd gone I discovered a reddish-brown stain on my panties and realized with dismay that my first period had begun. What an April Fool's Day joke on me! I had been told some months before about menstruation, but did not expect it before I was twelve. Mother had said that she was twelve and a half when hers began.

My immediate problem was that I was not prepared with the necessary equipment; so I folded up yards of toilet paper and placed it in my panties. Keeping this unsecured padding in place was difficult. It made me want to avoid all unnecessary activity. When my friends came by, I sent them away with a false excuse about having to stay home all day.

Then I took my book and carefully walked outside to a favorite spot; a flagstone fire circle where we sometimes had picnics. Although visible from the house, it was surrounded by trees and away from the street. I was hidden from my friends there.

I intended to read and remain as immobile as possible until Mother returned, but I was too upset by this new intrusion on my childhood to concentrate on the book. I remember sitting there quietly for a long time—wishing it were not happening—wishing my body would keep on being a child—feeling that it, too, had betrayed me by shoving me into the maturity I dreaded.

Eventually I went indoors to check the padding. I passed by the kitchen where Polly was working and she looked at me quietly. Her kind eyes invited my confidence. But I couldn't bring myself to tell her and ask her assistance. She must have sensed my distress; must have wondered why I sent my friends away; must have watched me sitting with my closed book beside me. She didn't ask any questions—she was just there for me if I needed her. I did need her, but I felt shy and sad and didn't know how to put it into words.

That evening after the family returned and Polly had gone home, I was still making pad-check trips to the bathroom—unable to tell Mother while my brothers were still running around. Finally we were all sent to bed and my parents were relaxing in the living room. I knew the time had come. I couldn't risk staining the sheets and much as I dreaded disclosing such an intimate problem, my mother had to be told.

When I appeared at the arched entrance to the living room and asked if she could come upstairs for a moment, my father exploded:

"What are you doing down here? Go to bed! Mother is tired. You can wait until morning to tell her whatever it is!"

His anger made it more difficult for me to insist, and her to respond, than it already was. By the time he calmed down and she accompanied me upstairs, the day's stresses had pushed me to tears, but I couldn't let myself cry. I knew that would upset her and further infuriate him.

Mother was as dismayed with my news as I had been that morning. "Now it's possible for you to have a baby!" she wailed. But she rallied, and helped me adjust the belt and napkin. I was acutely embarrassed, despite my relief in discarding the unreliable tissues.

Although that difficult first day and evening were never discussed with me again, I can't help speculating about my parent's conversation when Mother returned to the living room. Poor Mother— so tortured by fears that Dad's abuses had magnified.

From then on, life once a month was very different. I hated all the restrictions placed on my activities. To have to forego horseback riding and swimming for several days at a time was frustrating. I was also cautioned not to "belly-flop" on my Flexible Flyer sled. My protests, "Now it's no fun!" were ignored. Since boys weren't similarly limited by their maturing bodies, I felt the whole process of growing up was extremely unfair.

My mental picture of me at this age was of a stormy, bewildered little girl being dragged into womanhood—kicking and screaming all the way. I not only felt unsafe with Dad, I distrusted my own emerging sexual feelings and knew that Mother distrusted them as well.

There seemed to be a giant unseen force operating, to sabotage what little childhood I had left, and fling me into vast, unknown dangers. I was scared and angry.

As my body developed, my father's interest in it ended. He soon confined his sexual pre-occupation to comments, questions and innuendoes. I had no way of knowing that my sense of partial release was due to only partial reality. I was not free.

6

AS THE TWIG IS BENT

Summer 1932

The first time I heard about an adult who molested children I was twelve. He was an employee of my uncle's. My nine-year-old cousin told me that the man took her and her friend into a shed, where he exposed himself. I don't believe he touched the girls, but he wanted them to touch him. My cousin told her father; the man was fired and left town.

Although the circumstances were different from my experience, when I heard about hers the familiar leaden feeling returned in the pit of my stomach. I knew she wasn't making it up. But I pushed the feelings away and didn't tell her about Dad. However, after hearing about the other man, my gnawing curiosity and confusion didn't give me any peace.

Our two families were spending the summer at our grandfather's hotel. One evening, while the parents were at dinner, my years of turmoil finally thrust their way out. We (three girls and four boys) dared each other to shed our pajama bottoms. There followed giggling and tickling—unexpectedly exciting—until our parents returned and caught us.

Since I was the oldest, I was extremely embarrassed, felt responsible and expected to be punished. To my surprise, Dad took me to a riding stable the next morning and engaged two horses.

Why is he giving me this favorite treat?

As we rode along a quiet country lane, his companionable manner puzzled me. I was certain he planned to scold and wasn't prepared for anything else. I wished he would just get it over with.

Soon he had me canter ahead while he followed. It was a cool summer day—perfect for riding—but I was too apprehensive to enjoy it. When I slowed to a walk and dropped back beside him he said,

"You're such a good rider, I want you to have a horse of your own some day."

"I've always wanted one," I dared to respond.

But I've been too bad. Why isn't he angry with me?"

"I know you're old enough to take care of one; I hope we can manage it somehow."

*Could he mean this? Why is he being nice when I feel
so ashamed?*

Suddenly the cheerful expression became his hated leer of conspiracy.

*Oh no! Not his dirty side! When is he going to
bawl me out?*

Grinning slyly, he asked, "How could you get caught up in that nonsense with the kids last night?"

I can't answer him. I don't know.

Ignoring my silence, he continued gleefully, "Boy, it sure created a furor with the mothers! They were really upset."

*He's not angry at all. He thinks it was funny!
I feel awful.*

Determined not to cry, I choked out, "I wish it hadn't happened."

"Don't misunderstand," he went on. "They were shocked and are cross with you, but I'm not. It's just that I thought you knew you shouldn't do those things with your cousins and brothers."

"I do know it's wrong. I don't know why I did it."

*He knows it was fun and felt weird. But I hate those
feelings now. I hope they never come back!*

"Well," he said, "You surprised us, but I talked some sense into Mother afterward. She worries about you, but she'll get over this."

Following that ride/talk I still felt ashamed of myself and confused about Dad. My inability to resist the sexplay was even more ominous. It scared me. I avoided Mother, especially her unhappy eyes. She stared at me and didn't talk. I wondered why I wasn't even rebuked. I felt so much worse about what I had done than I did about the things for which I was usually punished. None of it made sense. I longed to recapture the innocent relationship with my cousins that I'd had before. I also wished that I hadn't given my brothers more reason to disrespect me. I felt abandoned by everyone.

To my relief, Mother eventually recovered and seemed herself again. Later she and I took a long trip with the other family. I really enjoyed seeing new places. It also gave me the chance to show that I could still relate responsibly with my cousins. But the chasm between my brothers and me only widened. We buried the incident between us but we never forgot it.

Our "happy family," circa 1932. Seated on the arm of Dad's chair, my smile covers my confusion about being "special" to him. Almost prophetically, the grouping reflects the basic structure of our early relationships, which continued quite unchanged as we grew up.

Struggles with inner pain took many forms. I often felt like a firecracker with a very short fuse. The least affront could still set me off. At other times, I felt frightened and lonely. Although these feelings were heightened when with the family, the teachers at school knew what to do. They managed to more or less civilize and encourage me during the five years that I was there.

One of my favorite teachers was Miss Dee. She taught sixth grade. She was quite a large lady who appeared understanding, strong and wise. She awed me when I first came to the school, but her broad smile disarmed my fear of her. One day when I was nine, she stopped me in the corridor to compliment me on my new dress. I felt that I'd just been knighted by a queen.

By the time I had finished fifth grade, my awe had turned to respect and I looked forward to being in her class the following year. Unfortunately for us, she went to France and we had a substitute teacher. I misbehaved most of the time.

The next year Miss Dee was back—teaching sixth grade and our small seventh grade class as well. She was full of interesting ways for us to explore and learn. It was like an adventure. We organized the Student Council and I was elected Chairman. I appreciated the honor, a tangible expression of regard by my schoolmates.

Then in the spring Miss Dee had to be away for a couple of weeks and we had another substitute. I promptly reverted to my disruptive tactics, encouraged the others to join me and made her life miserable. I thought I was getting away with it because no one said anything.

One afternoon soon after Miss Dee returned, the school principal paid our class a visit. This was very unusual. She came to the front of the room and said she wanted to talk to us. Miss Dee went over to her desk and sat down, turned at an angle so she could watch the principal and us at the same time. She looked very grave.

The principal told us that our behavior toward the other teacher had been deplorable and that we must never let that happen again. As I stared down at the top of my desk and privately reflected that I was the ringleader, the principal spoke my name. My whole body stiffened. I had to look up—had to face her.

"Under the circumstances, Barbara, you do not deserve your position as Chairman of the Council."

As soon as I dared, I looked over at Miss Dee. Her face was impassive as she met my eyes. She didn't look angry at me.

"I am removing you from that office, effective immediately," the principal continued. "You may be able to earn it back, but it's up to you to make the effort."

Then she left the room. No one spoke. Not even Miss Dee. However, I could feel a strong thread of understanding from her that was like Polly's when I was under a cloud at home. I knew she didn't condone my misbehavior, but in a way she didn't fully blame me.

We went on with our lesson and after class the others rushed to tell me they were sorry I had gotten into trouble. They said they felt they had been part of it. I knew I had led them, but it felt good to know they still liked me. Outwardly, I shrugged my shoulders and bluffed that I didn't care about being demoted. I don't remember whether I ever earned my way back on the Council.

But the teachers knew I did care and found ways to cut through my shell. Different ones would take the time to talk with me alone when I lost my temper. I knew they were trying to help me overcome my troublesome behavior. And they were also trying to make me aware of my creative potential. They didn't know the hidden source of my trouble, but they did everything they could to bring out my potential.

At the beginning of eighth grade, a new family with four children entered the school. The Johnsons were similar to our family in having three boys and a girl, but their girl was the youngest and in the first grade. Their oldest boy, Kurt, was the tallest in the school. He was in my class. By that time I had outgrown battling with the boys. I was feeling less cheated about being a girl. I wanted to be thought of more as a sports-loving person, welcome on any team, than a tough tomboy. I was working hard to control my temper.

Kurt sensed my suppressed volatility, though, and soon found a way to tease me and attract my attention. Every day when we were out of the classroom, he sneaked back in and placed my chair at the desk of a boy he knew I disliked. When I returned and found it, I became angry. But I didn't know who was moving it. Eventually I realized Kurt was the culprit and wrote him a blistering note. I threatened him with the direst of consequences if he moved my chair again. This brought a one-word note from him—"Snicker" was all it said. I felt ridiculed and furious. But I also felt powerless against a classmate for the first time. His hands were huge. I knew he was strong. I swallowed my pride and we became pals.

Soon our parents discovered they had common interests and their friendship grew as well. It was the middle of the Depression—a crucial time for them. Dad had undergone back surgery and now had digestive problems, requiring a special diet. Sometimes he was too ill to go to work for several days.

Business was plummeting for both fathers and they wanted to leave the Chicago area. They hoped to create better lives for all of us in the country.

Early the following year the two fathers found a small ranch on Sonoma Mountain in northern California. It had chickens and goats, a vegetable garden, some old fruit trees, a pretty house with flowers around it, and a small cottage. A grove of redwoods graced the northern end of the rolling pastureland. We were elated.

The Johnsons would have the original home and their boys would have the cottage. We would have a home designed by Dad, and built on a knoll overlooking the valley; with a cabin for my brothers nearby. And Dad promised me a horse of my very own!

PART TWO

"Adolescence is the last stop before womanhood. All of a girl's experiences from her childhood begin to converge and to form who she will become as an adult....

"When there is physical and/or sexual abuse as well, the impact on the child's development and self-esteem is even more devastating."

Dr. Susan Forward
MEN WHO HATE WOMEN AND THE WOMEN WHO LOVE THEM

TRANSITION

June 1934

Our trek to California was an exciting adventure. Mr. Johnson (whom we called Uncle Will), returned to Illinois to pilot the two cars, two mothers and eight children westward. It took ten days.

Aside from the journey itself, one factor made a strong impact on me. Kurt seemed to grow up overnight. At age fourteen he obtained a special driver's license and did much of the driving on that two thousand mile trip. Although I was only two months younger, my position was far beneath his. No one depended on me for anything. But his quiet assistance to the adults gave him influence over his siblings that even extended to disciplining them. It set him apart—only a trifle below the prestige accorded our parents.

Because Alice, my best friend in Illinois, had an older brother that I liked, Kurt's role was an acceptable one. I looked up to him. I sought his attention and longed for his approval. However, our friendship was changing. The walks we had enjoyed in Illinois were supplanted by his endless tinkering with various old cars. We occasionally took hikes, but our sense of companionship waned as we became more like siblings ourselves.

When we moved to California we began a new way of life. I loved being on the Ranch and learning what we needed to know to make it succeed. At first I didn't miss the friends I'd left behind. However, there were some losses that were difficult to understand and accept. For example, a letter from Dad written that spring, set the stage for a crushing disappointment. It turned up recently in a box of old photographs. More than fifty years later I realized it contained hidden messages which had eluded the child-me. But in the glare of present awareness, Dad's real intentions when he wrote are clearly apparent.

Glen Ellen, 3/18/34

Dearest Babs

Your nice long letters are very much appreciated because they give me a better picture of what you kids are all doing than I get from anyone else and if you can squeeze in time both Uncle Will and I would be glad to hear about the goings on. I got quite a kick out of your making a dress with Polly's able guidance. Gee, Babs, you're going to be crazy about it here on the ranch. Yesterday a girl from the ranch below rode over on her horse and Katie (the daughter of the former owners, who still live here) went out and caught her horse, saddled it and they went off together for the afternoon. She has a nice little horse and they would like me to buy it, but I learned by accident it is 15 years old so I don't believe you want her—besides they want too much for it. We have been dickering a long time about the goats and finally yesterday we bought the whole herd (except the Billy kids—baby males), one cream separator and an auto truck thrown in. All for a ridiculously low price. We now have—

1) 9 full grown nannies	We get up every morning at 6 and help milk.
2) 4 young nannies	
3) 1 full grown billy	At first our hands got
4) 2 nanny kids	awfully tired because the
5) 1 cream separator	muscles of our hands had
6) 1 auto truck	to become accustomed to the practice of milking. We are
added to our farm.	getting better each day.

This afternoon we had another cute little nanny added to the flock. As I am writing she is now 6 hours, 5 minutes and 31 seconds old. Next week I hope to have some pictures to send you of the nanny kids—Empress Josephine, Queen Christina and Amelia Earhart, respectively. Amelia is my special pet and follows me around like a dog. They will be still small when you get out here.

Beautiful blue iris are all in bloom now bordering the walks and driveway. Roses are just starting to bloom and many other kinds of flowers are getting ready for Spring. I picked a handful of strawberries yesterday. Uncle Will's peas which he planted only a week ago are sprouting. How I wish I could go on and on writing the thousand and one little incidents of the day, but I can't. I must stop and write Mother and after that many other letters. The letters to you kids and Mother are the "for fun" letters; after that are the "have to's."

Love and a big hug my dear from Dad

This is how the letter reads to me now: His first sentence was written to stir my pride in his regard for me and to enhance my confidence in our "special" relationship. He then tied his enthusiasm for the Ranch to his earlier promise of a horse. While whetting my hopes to go riding with the neighbor girls, he informed me that he wasn't buying the horse that was already there. Instead he let me assume I would have a younger one.

Then he abruptly switched to describing the goats in elaborate and appealing detail. He concluded by saying that he had written to me first, before Mother, which promoted my young girl's fantasy—I still held the inside edge in his heart. This once-treasured letter reveals his skill in strengthening his hold, while bending me to accept a major letdown. Because he counted on our help with the chores, he wanted to turn my horse dreams into enjoyment of the goats as pets. So he deliberately "set me up." He had no intention of keeping his promise—ever.

At first I was crushed with disappointment and couldn't believe the reason Dad gave—insufficient pasture for goats and a horse—since there had been enough for all of them before we came. Aware of my letdown, he made arrangements for me to ride horses at the nearby Jack London Ranch. It was fun to be there, close to the horses, and I went as often as possible.

At home I adopted two frisky and amusing goat twins as my own. Besides milking the nannies, I helped in the delivery of difficult births, and cared for some through bouts of mastitis. Several of my "patients" became my pets. They waited for me after school like loyal companions, and helped relieve my longing for a horse.

But in the world of people, life often seemed lonely. There was no one in my corner at home, as Polly had been. And at high school I felt different from the others in appearance and background. They had grown up on farms or in a small town, and were disappointed when I didn't know as much about Al Capone as they did. "You mean you never saw him when you were in Chicago?"

I soon discovered that entering the high school physical education program was like entering a foreign arena. Not only were boys and girls separated for sports, but the girls had to play by different rules. I didn't miss playing with the boys—I missed playing hard, using skills and running fast. Girls' basketball was too crowded to be fun, with nine players on a team. And there was no soccer at all. To compensate for these disappointments, I devoted myself to my studies and for two years was a member of the California Scholarship Federation.

All my brothers were having their teeth straightened. My front teeth were crooked too, and I wanted them to be fixed, as much as I longed for curly hair. I asked if I could have braces like theirs, but because I sucked my thumb when I was little, Mother said I had brought my crooked teeth upon myself. "You'll just have to live with them," she told me. I practiced trying not to smile, so they wouldn't show, but I couldn't keep them covered.

My brothers also had their eyes tested and received glasses. Mine were not tested until an alert high school teacher said they looked strained, and urged me to have them examined. Glasses were then prescribed. Ordinarily I would not have wanted them, or braces on my teeth, for they can be distracting and uncomfortable. But, to me, discomfort was unimportant. It was the attention to personal needs that I yearned for, and which they represented.

It hurt to see such excellent care taken of my brothers' teeth and vision, while mine went unnoticed.

We lived more than ten miles from school and returned home promptly each day to chores and homework. There was no time for socializing with friends as we had done in Illinois, but I felt more secure on the Ranch. It was more of a refuge than the homes in Illinois had ever been.

Sharing it with another family promoted this safe feeling because it expanded our family's activities with others. We lived in separate houses, but our work and recreation were cooperatively planned. This helped diffuse my uncomfortable relationships at home. And animosity toward my brothers faded as we involved ourselves in our new surroundings.

While starting a fire in my wood stove recently, I remembered that I learned how from my parents. I learned even more through watching them interact while fire-building.

Dad was meticulous in his preparations. The ashes were carefully pushed to the sides, to allow an air passage beneath. He would leave a thin layer of ash on the fireplace floor. Then he rolled newspaper into sticks, arranged kindling cross-hatch fashion on top, and finally all would be ready for the touch of the match. His care would reward him with splendid flames. After a few moments he would add the oak logs which warmed the room.

Occasionally he was outside when Mother wanted a fire. Her technique was less complicated. But if he happened to come in before she had it going, he couldn't allow her non-method to happen. He would remake it with a cheerful, "Here, Dearie, let me do it." As she moved aside, he proved once again that this was man's domain. To him, apparently, women were incapable of building fires.

Sometimes Mother succeeded in getting a fire started before he came in. And she was jubilant. She couldn't resist crowing gleefully, as the crackling logs proved her skill. I wish I had learned then the lesson their behavior imparted—that while his method always worked, hers usually did too, whenever he let her complete it.

I was dismayed when the cooperative, adventurous courage Mother and Dad shared was clouded by disguised hostilities. For example, Dad insisted in her presence that we respect Mother, while privately he demeaned her. When he advised my brothers to "Do whatever you're going to do, but don't tell your mother," he made deceiving her the rule. We were all conditioned to hold these ambiguous attitudes, through the double messages in his admonitions.

Mother, too, taxed their relationship by allowing her anxieties full rein, and badgering Dad about her concerns; such as urging him to change his clothes before going to town. Often he retaliated in fury. Their battles were noisy, with yelling, the banging of doors, and a number of dramatic exits; but when they were angry they never touched each other.

One time during that first summer when I was fourteen, Dad's rage was directed at me. He thought I had given Mother a disrespectful look, and he suddenly grabbed me. I broke free—ran outside. He followed and chased me around the Ranch as I tried to outrun him. Bobby, terrified, began screaming over and over, "Daddy's killing Barbara!" When Dad finally did catch me, he was so angry I thought he would kill me. He spanked me as hard as he could in front of everyone.

Later, in response to Bobby's terror he asked, "Can't a father spank his own daughter?" He could and did, but it brought me close to hating him for the first time in my life.

When we moved to California I hoped to escape forever from my bruised childhood. But it was not to be. The thrill of going West and the friendship of the other family were clouded by the inner wounds which would not heal: my sense of confusion, uncleanness, and shame. In my private world they separated me from everyone I knew and cared for—whose love and respect I craved—especially from Kurt and his family.

He and I were the evening goat-milkers and soon learned the routine and idiosyncrasies of these amusing animals. Sometimes we disagreed about the chores and tried to leave the more difficult ones for the other person.

One evening after I had responded angrily to the way he out-witted me, he chased me out of the barn where he caught me and spanked me in front of the surprised younger children. Suddenly humiliated, I became afraid of him.

I wasn't afraid of his rage, as I had been with Dad, because he seemed to be in control—enjoying himself and my humiliation; but I was aware of his strength, through the pain in my arms when he gripped them and threw me down across his knees. Terrified by his obvious pleasure in hurting me, and shocked by this glimpse of cruelty, my courage to fight back quickly evaporated. Since his retaliation was so out of proportion to the fuss in the barn that prompted it, I realize now that his usually quiet, responsible manner concealed a fearsome rage.

There was really no excuse for Kurt to punish any of us. But since he had assumed a semi-parental role with his siblings, he felt confident in his right to expand it to me; only I triggered a violence that day that fortunately the younger children had been spared. I don't recall that he was ever deterred in his practice of "discipline" by any of our parents.

With the onset of puberty, I had become highly preoccupied with emotions and sensations that I didn't understand. I wondered about boys and fantasized about them as romantic partners. Sexual activity did not intrude on these early daydreams—just warm feelings of being close.

Part of me was apprehensive about how a boy would expect me to behave if we were alone; part of me was terrified by the idea of anyone touching me; part of me was worried that no one would want to touch me because I was still lumpy, ugly and unappealing in every way; and all of me felt fearful about the slightest sexual awareness that I experienced spontaneously now and then.

I sensed that no matter how hard Mother tried to instill the proper attitudes and restraints in me, I would never be able to control my sexual responses. Much as I squirmed at the thought, I couldn't avoid feeling that I was flawed beyond redemption.

Mother reinforced this misplaced sense of guilt with her obsessive anxieties. They clouded my life like heavy smog. Her variety of approaches to expressing her concerns was endless, but they were always a repetition of what I'd already heard. Only the words were changed—the messages were the same:

Sexual feelings are dangerous—like anger. Until you are married it's best to ignore (deny) them;

Hand-holding should be avoided because it can lead from awareness to arousal;

Arousal should only be shared by married adults;

Intercourse should never be indulged in for purely sensual pleasure;

The appropriate sexual goal for which couples should strive, is one in which emphasis is on a higher level of communion than just the physical aspect of intercourse.

Because I had been hearing all this since I was a small child—in tandem with her endless prying (not to mention Dad's duplicity)—her cautions had lost any effectiveness they might have had. But part of me believed her. Physical contact could lead to serious problems. However, I wished with all my heart she would think of some of the other aspects of me and my new friends to talk about. I felt as though she had no interest in me, or them, as total human beings. But I never told her. Only now do I realize why I didn't let her know that I hated these talks. I felt so guilty about the incest and so confused about my feelings, I didn't dare tell her anything.

Mother never knew that I had overheard the conversation with her friend several years before. One day when she came into my room, she shut the door and I knew she was going to ask me about sex. I thought she had my friends on her mind, so wasn't prepared to have her blurt out,

"I know that Dad showed you about your body when you were much younger. What I want to know is if you think it was a good idea. Do you think it harmed you in any way to learn all that?"

"I don't know."

"Please, try to remember. Tell me what you think about it, now that you're older."

"Mom, I really don't know."

And I hate to remember.

"I've been worried about it for a long time. I was afraid it was bad for you, but I wasn't sure. Now, I want you to tell me."

"Please—I can't talk about it."

This was the first of many similar non-discussions about the incest, as she continued to question me for the rest of her life. She was too intelligent not to recognize my distress when she pressed me. She simply chose to ignore my feelings and to badger me for the reassurance I was unable to offer.

Somehow I got caught up in her fears for me and felt increasingly unsure of myself. It might be thought that this awareness of character weakness (which I assumed "nice girls" didn't have), should have protected me from anyone's overtures. But I knew nothing about resisting them. The only way I had survived sexual advances was by slipping into numbness. It was all I knew. Now in my longing to be cared for, I was drawn (in spite of my fears) to thinking about some of the boys at school.

My first crushes were secret. I lived on imagined warmth; but the attraction was basic and strong. It was a relief to discover that when my thoughts were crowded with fantasies, there was no room for sexual memories of my dad. I could escape—into a safe new world—the world of daydreams. And the unsuspecting boys retained all the innocence I wanted for myself.

By the time I was fifteen, I had concluded that submissiveness to both my parents was the only way to survive. About a year before, a teacher friend had warned Mother that fifteen-year-old girls were usually moody and difficult. So when I reached that dreaded age, Mother was surprised. She happily told her friends (in my presence), that although I had been an awful child, now at last I was no problem at all.

One afternoon when I returned from school, I was met by Mother in the patio outside the house. She looked nervous and agitated as she told me,

"Some very old friends are here and they want to meet you. But Dad has been bragging that you are still so unspoiled, you don't even wear makeup. I didn't dare say that you wear a little lipstick."

*My neck is getting warm—I can't stop blushing. I
wonder if she has noticed that I pluck my eyebrows too.*

"What do you want me to do.?" I asked.

Then I realized that her self-appointed mission was to intercept me before I was seen by anyone; so that I could remove the lipstick. Still blushing, I complied without question. It never occurred to me that what I did to my face was my personal right, even if it embarrassed Dad. I had finally become a well-mannered daughter and Mother didn't want anything to shatter this image.

Part of my sex education took place in the shower room at school. This steamy, drab place was far from glamorous. There was a row of stalls where we showered, dried, and tried to don underclothes without getting them wet on the cold concrete floor. Against the opposite wall were long benches where we sat to put on our shoes. We crowded before the one mirror at the end of the room to comb our hair.

One morning in this room, soon after Christmas vacation, the older girls were discussing the gifts they'd received. While I dressed and discreetly watched them apply makeup, one teased the other, saying, "Guess what my boyfriend gave me for Christmas."

I was astonished when she said that it was a pair of black lace panties. The other girl then asked the same question that had popped into my mind,

"What did your mother say?"

"She laughed!"

To picture my own mother in this unlikely situation was impossible; even the thought was absurd. I could imagine the improper relationship that the girl had with her boyfriend. But I couldn't picture any mother laughing if her unmarried daughter received such a gift from a boyfriend—especially on Christmas—in front of her family.

To me, this whole scene was amazing. The inferences about other families' relationships and standards shocked me. While I puritanically didn't approve of it, I was intrigued by the implied permissiveness it revealed. How could our two mothers be so different? Did my mother really know what she was talking about, I found myself wondering.

I started observing other families more carefully. I looked for clues to other parents' attitudes and compared other parents with mine. I began to feel that Mother and Dad were different from others, and not necessarily always right.

"Children learn from the important adults in their lives how to have a significant human relationship. Once a person has learned how to have a relationship with other people, then the sexual component can be added as a special expression of a special relationship. If the parents or significant adults are sexual with the child, the young person will always have difficulty sorting out sexuality and relationship."

Patrick Carnes, Ph.D.
OUT OF THE SHADOWS

8

TURMOIL

Summer 1936

I am vacationing with my cousins and their friends at Lake Tahoe. I watch them tease each other good-naturedly, and I envy them their ease together. But I don't know how to share it.

I am also acutely aware of my body. Its intrusive sensations distract and trouble me, but I try to appear primly above interest in boy-girl behavior, while I hope to appear worldly wise about it. I am neither. I have no idea what is expected of me when I am alone with one of the boys. Tim, a friend of my cousin's, is being nice to me. I like him and hope he likes me too.

Yesterday afternoon I was thrilled when he invited me for a boat ride. We went to the island in the middle of Emerald Bay, got out of the boat and pulled the bow up onto the shore. Then we started hiking up the path. I didn't know what to expect, and became uneasy. When we reached the top, we were all alone on this small island—surrounded by clear, blue-green water, lapping gently on the rocky shore below.

I wanted to feel relaxed and confident, but I felt awkward and afraid. I wasn't afraid of Tim—I was afraid of myself. I knew he was going to discover that I wasn't funny and smart like the other girls and be disappointed.

We paused, side by side—watching the birds we had startled as we approached, soar high across the water. Then Tim broke the silence.

"I'm really glad I'm in college now," he said. "Where do you plan to go when you graduate?"

When I told him I didn't know, he went on to say that it was far more interesting than high school. I barely heard him. My thoughts had tumbled back to the car-ride with Dad five years before—when he warned me about college boys. Now it's happening and my inner voice pleads—

Oh no! Not that awful song about "bulls with their long red bars." Please don't sing it—Please be nice to me— Please believe I'm a good girl.

He didn't sing that song; he sang another one. We were still standing side by side, looking out over the water—not touching.

"Then put her in the corner
And hold her tight like this,
And put your arms around her waist
And on her lips a kiss.
And if she starts to murmur
Or if she starts to cry,
Just tell her it's the sacred seal
Of old Phi Kappa Psi."

Well, Dad had said he'd sing a fraternity song and he did. It wasn't dirty, though, and even sounded tender to me. I wanted to be the girl with Tim's arm around my waist.

As we stood there quietly, I moved nearer to him. When his arm slipped behind me, I held my breath and didn't speak or move. Then, as I resumed breathing, he said, "You're a nice girl and you're very young. I don't know why I sang that song, because I'm not going to be romantic with you. It wouldn't be fair." I try to understand, as inner voice explains—

He doesn't think I'm pretty and bright like the other girls, so he's just being kind.

"You are the same age as my little sister," he went on, "and I can't think of you in any other way. Do you know what I'm trying to say?"

"Yes, I think so," I softly reply.

I feel sad, though. I don't need any more brothers. I want to be special to Tim, like a girlfriend. His arm feels good—so safe—so strong. I want to lean my head on his shoulder, but I know he doesn't want me to. I wish I was older.

When my relatives returned to their home near Santa Barbara, I went with them. There I met a young man who invited me to go to the movies one evening. Although my cousin advised me not to go, I went while Aunt Jane was out to dinner—without her permission. I don't remember what we saw, but on the way home he parked the car and reached over to take my hand. I felt a little frightened, but I let my hand stay in his.

Then he turned to face me and began to caress my neck and arm with his other hand. He was smiling. His touch was gentle and felt good—but wrong. I could feel myself melting inside and sliding—

*Oh—I wish he wasn't doing this, but I don't know
how to stop him. I don't want him to think I'm too
young—like his little sister.*

When he kissed me, he moved his hand down to my breast. Panic
rushes in—melting sensation disappears—rag-doll child-me gives up—
And I'm slipping on the mossy bottom of the swimming pool—Can't save myself—going under—drowning—blankness—

He stopped after the kiss, and had little to say on the way back
to my cousin's home. I was relieved, but felt rejected. I was also
ashamed afterwards around my relatives. They were doing everything
to give me a happy summer, and we all knew I had betrayed their trust.
When Aunt Jane scolded, I knew I had it coming.

After that I tried to act like my cousins as much as I could. I
listened to how they talked to each other and to their parents. I was
learning a lot. Their light-hearted humor expressed genuine affection
and it felt good to be with them—very different from being at home. I
never felt that I was one of them, though; I felt more like an admiring
observer.

That fall when I returned to Sonoma Valley High School, I was
pleasantly surprised. A boy named Marty began to talk with me more
than he ever had before. I liked him. He was an excellent student,
played in the school orchestra and band, and was also accomplished in
baseball, track and basketball. We had been in the same classes for two
years. Now he wanted to know me better. Every morning I could hardly
wait to get to school.

Our friendship developed with Marty's invitation to a noontime
walk on the unpaved country road beside the school. I felt self-
conscious, but as we sauntered along, his eyes suddenly twinkled as he
asked, "Do you like chicken?" In surprise, I answered, "Yes," to which
he suggested, "Grab a wing!" and proffered his bent arm toward me. I
laughed, put my hand through his arm and we began to "go together."

What a thrill it was to be chosen—to be special to someone! I
finally began to feel that I was joining the rest of the human race. As our
relationship continued, we shared some of our most private thoughts
and dreams. I had never been so happy.

He didn't have a car, so it wasn't easy to get together on
weekends, but when he managed it, we went for walks up Graham
Canyon—near the Ranch. Graham Creek rushed down beside a trail
that wound through stately redwood trees. There was a rustic foot-

bridge crossing the creek and quiet groves where we could have a picnic. We felt drawn together and private in these natural surroundings.

Even though we didn't share family secrets, we alluded to them, and this was enough to dispel our loneliness. I knew he cared about me. It was good to talk and listen to each other as friends, not lovers; and made our hugs seem a natural part of something special. But I was so starved for physical touching by someone who really appreciated me, that I soon yearned to move beyond our tender embraces. I knew nothing about drawing a line on our behavior. Fortunately, Marty did. Gently, and without hurting my feelings he dissuaded us both from losing control. He let me know through his eyes that he loved me while he said, "We can't, you know. We have to stop." I believe this close friendship nurtured us both and was strengthened by Marty's unusual wisdom.

He never let his lack of a car keep him from visiting me—especially when I was ill and missed school. Somehow he would find a way to come over and report the latest school news, even when I was hospitalized with the flu. But one ride he arranged led to an unexpected disaster.

It was a Saturday evening and we had gone to a dance in Sonoma. Kurt had taken those of us from the Ranch, including my brother Eric. Marty and I had met at the dance. He gave me a gardenia for my blue taffeta gown, and as we danced every dance I wished our date could go on forever. Marty did, too, so he asked a friend and his girl to take me home when it was over.

With Eric's promise not to tell Mother about my ride-change, we began the long drive home. I didn't know Marty's friends very well and it was fun to become acquainted while I was feeling so grown-up and at ease. But as we climbed up Sonoma Mountain, we noticed an unusual number of cars on the road, especially for that time of night.

Then, before we were in sight of the Ranch, our friend pulled the car off to the edge of the road and parked. I had not been in this kind of situation since the time I was visiting my cousins, but I wasn't afraid. I felt safe with Marty. However, we were both embarrassed. The other couple was older, and obviously more experienced.

When a car coming down the mountain stopped, I recognized the driver as a boy from high school. He called out to us, "Is Barbara in there?"

No one answered. Then he said, "Well, if you see her, tell her that her house is on fire. It's almost all burned down!"

We returned quickly to a conflagration, with everyone in the area involved in trying to stop it and save what they could. Since Eric was already home, it was impossible for me to sneak in and there was nothing left to sneak into. I thought the fire was so devastating my misdemeanor would seem minor at the time. But it was not overlooked. From then on my comings and goings were scrupulously monitored, and my dates caused Mother increasing anxiety.

Sometime during those middle high school years, I began associating menstrual cramps with punishment for sexual urgings. I enjoyed Marty's hugging and kissing which made me feel loved. But it also aroused deeper sensations that felt dangerous and spookily pleasant. When I encouraged their occurrence through kissing, I believed I was being sinful and the cramps that came later were my just penalty. I didn't know that these mysterious sexual responses were a normal part of being human.

To my surprise and relief, I discovered that writing provided an outlet for my feelings, and began to write passionate love-notes to Marty. He knew they expressed only my affection, but to others they could imply far more. When Mother went through my purse one day and read a note addressed to him, she believed the worst had already occurred. She was too upset to feel a shred of guilt for invading my privacy.

Instead of discussing it with me, however, she told Dad. This meant a walk/talk for us, on the trail up the canyon. I hated to go there with him. I didn't know they'd found the note, but I knew he was going to talk about sexual matters. When he quoted the note, I was horrified; then too embarrassed by the exposure of my emotions to feel angry at Mother's intrusion—into my room, my drawer, my purse, my folded note. I just felt frightened, humiliated and dismayed.

What are they going to do next? Dad broke my Japanese box—now Mother goes into my purse. No safe hiding place—have to stop writing.

Even though I didn't expect Dad to believe that we had only kissed, I firmly denied "petting" with a clear conscience. However, his concern had more to do with my choice of friends than with my behavior. In Dad's eyes, Marty was a self-confident achiever that I would be unable to resist—like the college boys he warned me about when I was a child. I knew he was wrong about Marty, and tried to tell him. But he wouldn't listen. I felt he would never believe I was right about anything—especially a boyfriend.

Mother hoped I would not be serious about anyone until I had graduated from college. But I didn't feel I wanted to be that patient; or could afford to be that choosy. I was an outsider to Sonoma; I had never felt as though I belonged in my high school class—until this year.

When Dad concluded his remarks that day with, "Mother is going to keep on worrying unless you end your friendship with him," I was crushed, absolutely smashed flat.

"But we aren't doing anything bad! Please don't make me do that," I pleaded, "He's really my best friend."

"We have to think of Mother now. I want her to stop being upset about you. And she doesn't want you to be with him anymore."

The next day, as the school bus wound slowly through the valley to Sonoma, I wanted to get off at every stop and run away. I didn't know how I was going to tell Marty. When I came into the main hall and found him waiting with his cheery grin, it was too much. I broke down and he led me to a quiet corner, suddenly alarmed. He was stunned when I told him. We wanted to hold each other, but in school we couldn't, so we tried to find comfort in knowing we would still see each other there, and in hoping that my parents would later relent.

But after Dad's talk with me, Mother privately took the matter into her own hands. She was determined to sever our relationship completely; so she enlisted the aid of one of our teachers. When the teacher reported that we were still walking down the country road at noon, Mother demanded that we immediately stop "going together," even at school.

It was a devastating ultimatum. We still shared classes, so couldn't avoid each other—or the questions of our friends. We were miserable. We felt unfairly judged and sentenced, but we knew we were beaten since we lived so far apart and I couldn't escape surveillance.

By this time my grades had slipped and I was expected to bring them up, despite what had happened. It was the last straw. I felt my inner rage churning, but I pretended, both at home and at school, that it was over between us and that I didn't care. It was the only way to get Mother to leave me alone. I anguished privately, knowing that Marty had been hurt and felt angry too. He didn't understand what all the fuss was about—especially since he had never taken advantage of me in any way.

After that, the confused attempts at self restraint that I was learning from him began to disappear. I wanted to be treated like an adult and be my own boss. I wanted a relationship that included what I now thought of as adult behavior.

Some months later, when my next boyfriend, Richard, ventured beyond kissing, I always felt guilty, but I never felt irresponsible. I simply tried to meet his needs in the only way I knew. However, I was no longer open and free in my behavior because I had more reason to hide—from my friends, the school, and especially my family. As we became more physically intimate, though, we sometimes took chances on being discovered; and I found I enjoyed an odd thrill in knowing we were deceiving my parents.

Strangely, although this relationship was far more threatening to my future than the one with Marty, my parents did not object. I never understood why. But I didn't dare ask—I was too relieved—and feared another loss more than anything in the world. I couldn't bear to be alone again.

I don't remember my first experience of intercourse. I have no idea when or where it occurred, or the circumstances leading up to it. I assume this is a guilt-caused memory block. I do know that when it happened, the only attempt at birth control I can remember was Richard's withdrawal. We weren't knowledgeable—we were lucky.

Neither of us was promiscuous. I just wanted to feel loved and safe with one person—the direct opposite of scary, hated incestuous assaults where I felt "done to," never "shared with."

Richard was new to our school and as consumed by his needs, as I was by mine. Although we had good times with our friends, often when we were alone he was troubled and unhappy. We talked a lot, but there was always a distance between us—an inability to confide in each other. I knew I couldn't lean on him, like I could with Marty. But I tried not to compare them. I dimly sensed that when Marty became lost to me, I became more lost than ever to my self.

So physical intimacy became a substitute for emotional intimacy, but it did not always lead to intercourse. It never led to orgasm for me. However, since I had heard very little about that phenomenon, I assumed it happened to wives when they conceived a baby. Maybe, I thought, it's what Mother referred to as the beautiful reward for waiting until marriage. If so, I had thrown away my chance to experience it. My arousal responses always faded soon after intercourse began and I just went numb. But I wasn't surprised. Sex, guilt and numbness were always intertwined. I didn't know that what I really hungered for was *being* loved, not *making* love.

Soon, I began to initiate romantic touching—to generate a warm response and also to achieve a sense of being in control. It never worked. I couldn't hold the line between affection and passion. On the other hand, when my boyfriend took the lead—the familiar pattern of easy submission always dictated my responses. I had learned all about how to initiate or submit and nothing about how to choose or refuse.

As time went on, the more I thought I cared for him, and showed it, the less I was able to care for myself. I felt ashamed and dishonest inside, no matter where I was or what I was doing. One of my brothers' teachers, who was a young man and friend of the family, came over to see us and I asked him to sign my autograph book. He was light-hearted and joked a lot and I expected him to write something funny. I only remember part of his message. It was: " ...and always maintain your integrity." I thanked him and after he left I looked up what integrity meant. Then I cried myself to sleep. His message had come too late.

During my senior year when I started looking for a college, I hoped to find a coeducational one that was far enough away to escape Mother's supervision. Richard had joined the Navy by then, so there was no reason to remain near home. When I visited my cousin's friend at Occidental College in southern California, I found it met my criteria. So I applied and was accepted.

The next problem was to figure out what course of study I wanted to pursue. With only confused impressions about what my body was for, I had enormous difficulty figuring out what my life was for. I don't remember discussing the future with my parents. But they didn't seem concerned about the career decisions I was trying to make. All I can recall Mother saying was that she didn't want me to become a nurse; which hadn't occurred to me. But perhaps her negative comments planted the seed that made nursing appeal to me later.

I had always enjoyed small children, so I thought I might be able to teach. To test my abilities I found work in a summer camp across the valley, my first real job. I was paid $35 a month, plus room and board, and I was thrilled. My independence seemed within reach.

The camp proved to be a rewarding experience. When it was over, I was encouraged by the director to continue my education and prepare for a teaching career. Now I looked forward to college and was eager to go.

September 1938.

Although I had a strong desire to be free of my family, I was not prepared to fly alone. As I settled into the freshman girls dorm, I felt like the ugly duckling from the country who had fallen into Swan Lake; that everyone else was wise to the ways of the world and knew how to relate.

In the dorm I got off to a painful start. I didn't know that the students supplied their own curtains and bedspreads, and I arrived (alone, via train), without them. We were told to prepare our rooms for an open house, so I measured my windows, took a streetcar to downtown Los Angeles, found a bedspread and material that didn't need lining; then hurried back to handsew through the night, four full length curtains—but I didn't make it. My windows were bare—the only ones uncurtained in the entire dorm of sixty girls.

The other freshman girls had fun at the mixers—informal dances in the student union. I went a few times because I liked to dance. But I was never asked to dance—not even once. I assumed that I must look too unsophisticated for the boys there and stopped going. Sometimes a classmate would ask me out for a walk or a daytime ride in his car. In my determination to remain true to Richard, I began by accepting these occasional dates and then telling them that I was "going with someone," as a guide to their expectations. It worked well to deter advances, but I was rarely asked out again.

As that year moved along, I became increasingly homesick for the known qualities of life on the Ranch and in the small high school I was accustomed to. Despite the strains at home, the uncertainties of college were even more stressful. I had looked forward to meeting new friends, who would enjoy outdoor fun, like hikes and picnics. But none of the girls were interested in exploring the nearby hills with me. Their attention was centered on boys, dates and clothes and, since I was uneasy when these subjects were discussed, I became a quiet (often bored) listener.

One time when I was lonely, I went to the campus post office. My box was empty. Tears suddenly rushed down my cheeks and, on turning away, I ran into another lonely, letterless freshman. He introduced himself and asked me to join him for a walk around the campus.

We talked about the homes we missed and soon felt better. After that we went out a number of times. He never pressed me for physical intimacies, and I felt at ease with him, but I missed being held and being told I was loved. It was hard not to have someone special at college.

During Christmas vacation when I was home, I met Jerry. He was attending the University of California at Davis and was two years older than me. He seemed reckless and carefree in his funny escapades with his car and I was attracted to his jaunty, rebellious streak (which I would have loved to imitate). The following spring, as my relationship with Richard faded despite our commitment to loyalty, Jerry and I began writing to each other. I soon discovered that underneath his light-hearted demeanor, he was also lonely and uncertain about his future. I understood this. We were both in college where we knew we should be, but we were both unhappy and we didn't know how to improve our situation.

There was one unusually positive experience during that year. Curiously, it occurred off-campus and I did not discuss it with anyone at the time. Through the Students' Christian Association, I volunteered one afternoon a week at a recreation center in an economically depressed part of the city.

The college forbade us to go there alone, but I couldn't find anyone to go with me on the only afternoon I had free. So I signed myself out to the library and went to the center every Friday—the entire school year. I tried to suppress my fear of the loiterers that I had to pass to get there, and walked as fast as I could, without running. They knew I was nervous and often teased me, especially when I flashed my Woolworth's wedding ring (bought for this situation), while adjusting my hat. The ring didn't fool anybody.

The elementary school girls with whom I worked were primarily from Mexican or Gypsy families, two groups that bore no love for each other. It was my first exposure to the hostilities existing between members of disadvantaged people. I learned that through shared activities, away from the prejudices endemic in their homes, they could drop their distrust and enjoy each other. We played games on the large flat roof of the building, sang songs around the piano, made up dances to different rhythms, as they took turns with cymbals and drums, and we all had juice and cookies together before they went home.

The pleasure of working with the creative leaders in that program and the enthusiasm of those responsive, often funny, little girls was well worth the scary walk to get there and the subterfuge at college. It was one afternoon each week in which I felt completely good about myself. No one there knew anything about me—or cared—and I knew they all liked to have me there.

When Dad came down in the spring, we climbed the hills behind the dorm that I had wanted to explore since I arrived. I hoped he wouldn't leer, or say anything off-color to spoil it. But I needn't have worried. While we rested at the top and enjoyed the view, he brought me up to date on family news and refrained entirely from sexual comments.

I was relieved to feel comfortable with him. Maybe now he would always treat me like an adult and I wouldn't ever feel dirty and awful when I was alone with him again. Despite everything he'd done, I still wanted to believe he was a wonderful father. So while his companionable approach during that visit enhanced this misperception, it also increased my homesickness. Later when he said, "We've missed you— I'll be glad when your summer vacation comes," I could hardly wait to return to the Ranch.

In June, as I packed my trunk and said good-bye to some of the girls in the dorm, I knew my education at Occidental College was over; even though I didn't know where I would be in September. It was enough to know I was finally going home. I wondered if I would see Jerry again.

9

ASPIRATIONS TO ASHES

June 1939

My return home did not bring the sense of security I had anticipated. My grandfather had been moved into my bedroom, so the only place left for me was the guest cabin at the other end of the Ranch. It was all by itself, over the hill near the redwoods, and many acres away from the main house. There was no telephone. Every night I heard strange sounds as I lay there in the dark—afraid. But I didn't tell anyone.

That summer while I worked in the children's camp, Jerry came to take me out in the evenings. After our letters, we welcomed this chance to become better acquainted and went for long drives in his car. We shared our dreams, our disappointments with college life, and our love for the country. We both longed to be out on our own, but I was afraid to try it alone. Jerry could hardly wait.

Sexual intimacies began to follow these serious conversations. They enhanced our two-against-the-world bond, and helped us believe we were really adults. We also believed that withdrawal made intercourse safe. Anyway, it was such a relief to feel close to someone, the risk seemed unimportant. Even the pleasure I had on my job and the camp director's encouragement to pursue a teaching career didn't inspire the self-restraint I needed.

I liked sex in its initial phases. I found the preliminary tenderness more enjoyable than the evolving responses, which brought on my familiar numbness. But I never associated this cloudy cessation of feeling with being molested. I assumed that it enveloped and subdued me because I had broken the rules in entering forbidden territory— intercourse before marriage. No doubt my guilty conscience contributed, but the sensation of sinking into numbness was a long-established response from childhood.

The guidance I received from Mother and Dad had dwelt on my choice of a mate, and they hadn't approved of my first two boyfriends as future husbands. But Jerry was different. They barely knew him. His mother and father were both professionals, though, and I believe that helped my parents accept him.

I enrolled in the nearby junior college, while Jerry decided not to return to college; he wanted only to farm. So late in August he drove up to Oregon to look into the possibilities there. When he returned in September (with two calves in the rumble seat of his roadster), I was attending classes—with only pretended interest in the subjects.

This nebulous attention soon waned as I was swept up in waves of nausea. I had missed my period by then and decided to tell Jerry that I thought I was pregnant.

"Oh my gosh, really? Well, don't worry—we'll figure out something." And I knew then that he would stand by me. Although we had no idea how, or when, or where, we assumed we would get married. We didn't know each other very well, but expecting our baby made us feel we knew each other well enough.

When I told my best girl friend from high school, I remember how happy I was. She was aghast and concerned, but she didn't let her feelings interfere with my need for someone to talk to—someone I could trust.

I also confided in a young married woman. She suggested that I have an abortion as she had done (before she was married), but I found this idea deeply distressing. Before my pregnancy was confirmed, she gave me some capsules prescribed by a physician friend of hers, which were supposed to bring on a delayed menstrual period. She said they would not harm the baby if I were pregnant. They had no effect. She renewed her efforts to persuade me to terminate the pregnancy, with reassurances that she had access to a qualified physician. But I couldn't even consider taking this step. My resistance did not stem from fear of pain or breaking the law. It came from the growing awareness that I wanted this baby and would go to any lengths to protect it. I hadn't tried to get pregnant to gain marriage—I drifted into it—with someone who seemed to need me as much as I needed him. We didn't feel lonely anymore.

But I was often engulfed in nausea and it was becoming impossible to conceal unpredictable bouts of vomiting. We realized that I wouldn't be able to hide my condition much longer, so we concentrated on how to tell our parents. We were very apprehensive about their reaction.

By then Jerry was working and living on the Jack London Ranch, across Graham Canyon from our Ranch, and we hoped that Dad would think well of him for having a steady job. We decided to tell Dad first.

The next evening when Jerry came over, we didn't go out. As planned, we stayed in the living room with the family—playing Anagrams with Grampa, then listening to *The Green Hornet* on the radio with my brothers, and finally telling them all good night as they went to bed. We waited awhile—then the time had come.

My parents slept in separate rooms, so after Mother was asleep, we tip-toed back to Dad's room. He was still reading, and looked up surprised as we entered. He didn't get angry when I told him, but he did look very grave. The only thing I can remember him saying was, "I'll have to find a way to tell your mother."

I didn't see Mother the next day until she had recovered her composure after hearing Dad's disastrous news. They had eaten a late breakfast and when I came into the kitchen, she was alone—standing in front of the open refrigerator, trying to remember what she had planned for dinner that night. She turned when she heard me and closed the refrigerator door.

> *Somehow a door always closes just before her talks—*
> *and I always feel cornered. She looks awful—she's*
> *been crying—it's my fault—*

"Oh Barbara, how could you?! After all I've tried to teach you, how could you let this happen?" Her drawn face was crumpling.

"It just did. I don't know what else to say,"

> *out loud, that is, 'cause I'm not really sorry. I want to*
> *be with Jerry. Now you're ashamed of me—but please*
> *don't cry—I need you—I'm scared—you said it hurt*
> *so much. I'm going to be brave—you'll see—*

"I just don't know what we're going to do," she agonized. "It's going to be so hard to tell everyone." Obviously, her concerns were on *her* immediate dilemma; my trip to the scary delivery table was many months away.

Our four parents, barely acquainted, deeply disappointed and unhappy, got together and planned our next steps. I don't recall that any alternatives to a secret wedding were even considered.

None of them mentioned abortion to me, which was an enormous relief. It would have been impossible to resist their pressure. Since I had never had any control over my body and what was done to it, I was terrified they would make this ultimate demand.* It was odd to

---

*I do not oppose abortion as an option to an unplanned pregnancy, but I believe that a woman should have the right to choose. Certainly no one lives with her decision more fully, or *permanently*, than she and her child. But as a non-assertive, guilt-ridden teenager, I could not have defended this conviction.

move from my mixed fear/hope of being pregnant, through the dreaded possibility of having my baby taken away, to the final clearcut certainty that *I wanted this baby.*

After that first morning, I don't recall any pre-marriage conversations with our mothers, but vividly remember the two questions put to me separately by our fathers. Dad took me for another walk/talk.

He said, "When we let you live in the cabin, we trusted you to behave yourself. I want to know if you betrayed our trust and abused the cabin. Is that where you got pregnant?"

How could he think that? I never wanted to be on the
Ranch with Jerry when we were by ourselves. We had
our own world—in the hills—miles away—

"We weren't there. We weren't anywhere on the Ranch," I managed to reply to this self-righteous, moralistic father I didn't recognize.

A few days later, Jerry's father was driving me down to their East Bay home and we were alone in the car. His calm, friendly manner put me at ease, and I hoped with all my heart he would like me. He wanted to know how long it had been since I had seen my previous boyfriend, and was reassured to learn that it had been many months. I'm certain he believed me. He never mentioned it again, was always warm and kind to me, and I became very fond of him.

He provided a lovely platinum band for Jerry to give me, set with tiny diamonds, and an early August wedding date engraved inside. Then Jerry and I went off alone to Carson City, Nevada. In a cotton print dress I had bought for $3.99 while in college, I became Jerry's wife. When we returned, our marriage was announced, giving the false date, which no one believed. But that was the usual way the matter was handled then and we went along with it.

I had no regrets that my education was short-circuited. Now I could stop that useless struggle and begin being a grownup with a family of my own. I was nineteen years old.

1939-40

There were many awkward and embarrassing occasions during that first year. Our mothers, each coping in her own way with friends and relatives, were often insensitive in their indirect reproach of me. I felt ashamed and wished the circumstances of our wedding had been conventional. I also felt guilty; it hurt to feel singled out for disgrace.

It was also upsetting to discover that I had become "fair game" for those who questioned our wedding date. Relatives, family friends and even mere acquaintances bluntly reminded me of social occasions I had attended without Jerry, and archly asked if we were married before those particular events. I always lied and said that we were, but that I felt obliged to honor the invitations, even though they didn't include him. These inquisitions continued for many years (the last one was twelve years later). And my sense of disgrace never ended. I believed then that it never would; that it was justly deserved punishment for immoral behavior.

Despite these painful feelings, nothing could dampen my joy of expectancy, not even fears about childbirth. Under the circumstances, though, I didn't want to appear too happy, so I assumed a decorous manner about the baby; while inside my heart was singing. I was delighted to be a wife—soon a mother.

When the time came for our baby to arrive, I was taken to the little country hospital which served the entire valley. In those days, before natural childbirth was an option, we were not encouraged to understand what to expect or how to participate. I had sent for government bulletins, wanting to learn as much as I could about what was happening inside me—what to anticipate, and do, during labor. But the bulletins dealt primarily with prenatal care and layette requirements. They were not very informative or instructive. Nothing prepared me for the long, frightening ordeal, during which I was medicated with Scopalomine so that I wouldn't remember the pain. I didn't awaken until my daughter was four hours old. I was alone in the room. I didn't know what had happened to my baby.

Her birth was extremely perilous to her. The cord was wrapped twice around her neck, forceps were used, and she was dusky on delivery. The doctor had great difficulty getting her to start breathing. A kind, concerned nurse, who assisted him, told me about it later and about how relieved she was when the baby was finally out of danger.

The next day I overheard a patient in the next room ask another nurse about me and express concern for me and the baby. Although this nurse had not attended the birth, she had seen me through an appendectomy and flu when I was in high school, and I always enjoyed her jolly manner. So I wasn't expecting her callous response.

"Oh, it wasn't as bad as she sounded. She's just a spoiled, sheltered girl, who's been babied!"

Suddenly my shame surrounding the baby's conception had extended to her birth, to be compounded by the scorn of a nurse I thought was compassionate. I assumed she was referring to my moans during the first hours, when I was doing my best to be brave. It was all I remembered. I didn't know that Scopalomine causes loss of emotional control, as well as memory, and that later on I had yelled for hours. I just wondered why my throat was so sore. But with the nurse's harsh words, I wanted to gather up my baby and flee—from everyone. I felt too ashamed to tell Jerry, sensing that he would have been unable to understand my desolate feelings, or drive them away. I was still nineteen.

We named our baby Susan—not after anyone—simply because we liked it. Mother came to see me the next day and was not pleased when I told her.

"It's not a good family name," she complained. "It's a servant's name. We used to have a maid called Susan."

She abruptly excused herself when the nurse came in—saying she wanted to view Susan in the nursery. I hoped she'd be pleased to see her at last. But on her return she laughed and blurted out sarcastically, "I hate to say this, Barbara, but she's not nearly as pretty as my babies were."

Why do you have to be so mean? She looks perfect to
me. Oh, Mother, do you have to spoil everything?—

Then I felt sad because she couldn't graciously welcome her first grandchild. She could only continue to punish me for disgracing the family.

I wanted to nurse Susan, but when I got home I didn't have enough milk, so the doctor had me supplement with a formula. As my milk decreased, Mother boasted that she had successfully nursed twin boys—each weighing over six pounds at birth. After a few weeks, I didn't have any milk at all, and felt totally under-equipped as a mother. What a poor way to start parenting a bright, adventurous, lively little girl. I tried not to think about Mother's unkind comparison of her own babies with mine (who had had such a tough time getting here), but I couldn't forget it.

A few weeks after Susan's birth we were able to move away from my parents' home to a seventy-five year old house we loved, on a ranch belonging to Jerry's family. It had been restored and Jerry's mother helped me furnish it. I happily began sewing curtains with ball fringes for the tall, old fashioned windows. At last I was experiencing the satisfactions and pleasures of making a home for my loved ones. When

Christmas came, Jerry gave me a pretty quilted robe with tiny flowers that he had chosen himself. I loved to wear it and felt more and more like a real wife.

One blustery Sunday in March, the wind blew wildly over the knoll on which our house stood. It whistled through the Italian cypress trees beside it, frequently laying them over. Jerry was working in a dairy some miles away. I built a fire in our fireplace and, with Susan playing in her pen, I sat on the sofa, writing in her baby book. That done, I began darning socks, listening to the radio, and feeling cozy.

By the time I put Susan down for her nap, the house was warm and I had let the fire go out. Then I checked the ashes, made certain there were no live coals, and stretched myself out on the sofa. Susan was already asleep. The wind was still howling and rattling the windows now and then, but I felt snug inside and drowsy.

Just before I closed my eyes to drift off, a puff of smoke blew down outside the windows. I couldn't believe it—the fire was out. I ran outside and found the entire roof ablaze. The howling sound was more than wind—it was roaring flames inside the chimney. A capricious waft of smoke had saved our lives.

I picked up Susan, called the fire department, and ran down the road to guide the trucks to our obscure entranceway. The first truck brought no water. The electrical pump wires to our well were quickly burned, which made our water unavailable. Our little home was doomed.

People came from everywhere and saved what they could. I stood in the orchard holding Susan—watching it burn to the ground—taking the robe and baby book with it. Somehow the cypress trees survived.

I wanted to wait there for Jerry to come home in order to soften his shock. I wanted him to see immediately that we were safe. But others said they would meet him, so once again I returned to the Ranch; and sank back into the dependency I thought was behind me. It felt as though I had never been away.

For months, visions of the fire were a bad dream that wouldn't end, while I took care of Susan and waited for the trance I was in to break. Jerry and I went back to the cabin, but it wasn't the same. Shattered and confused, he tried to find words for our feelings.

"I'm very thankful to have you and Susan safe," he said, "but we lost more than our home in that fire." And so we did.

73

10

AFTERMATH

Spring 1941

Our marriage was more fragile than we realized, because after the fire we couldn't recapture our sense of mutual sharing. Jerry was away for days, even weeks, at a time. No longer working in dairies, he began hauling lumber from northern California to the Bay Area. As his struggles to succeed generated mounting financial risks, my fears for our future pushed us even further apart.

I knew that one cause of his long absences was his drive to be his own boss, but I was lonely for him and often felt abandoned. I also felt guilty because I believed then that Susan and I were the main reason he worked so hard. When our families began questioning his judgment, I tried to reassure them, but my anxieties only deepened.

Sometimes while he was away, I would take Susan back to the Ranch for a day or two. We had a car by then and the visits provided a welcome change of scene for both of us. At fifteen months she was adventurous and eager to explore her surroundings, while maintaining a tight grip on a ragged, faded corner of pink baby blanket—her "banky."

She slept with it and always carried it with her while she played. When it was washed, she stood beneath the clothesline—waiting, sometimes sobbing, until it was dry and returned to her. We couldn't distract her from her vigil.

One day while we were at the Ranch, Dad took her with him for a trip to town and when they returned she realized her hands were empty. Her "banky" was nowhere to be found in the truck they had been riding in. That evening we tried to soothe her by providing a substitute—to no avail. She cried herself to sleep.

Several days later she was riding with me on the same winding country road, several miles from the Ranch. As we crossed a bridge, she was suddenly excited and pointed out the car window. "Dere's a banky!" she joyfully cried. I stopped the car. We scrambled down the bank beside the creek, where she retrieved her beloved scrap of security. It was in a spot well-hidden from the road. As I carried her back up the bank, I marvelled at her memory of the location, but couldn't help wondering what had caused her to leave behind her constant companion. She was too little to tell me.

At the time I didn't think the incident was significant, although I never forgot it. Even now it remains a mystery. But the clues are strong and they don't go away.

After World War II was underway, we moved about thirty miles to Larkspur in Marin County. I didn't know anyone there and felt more isolated than I had when we lived in the country. I tried to make friends and volunteered to help the war effort through the Red Cross. But they said they couldn't use me, because I would be bringing my child. So I took long walks with Susan around that scenic community at the foot of Mt. Tamalpais, while knowing I would never belong there.

Eventually, overwhelmed by loneliness and hunger for someone to want to be with me, I turned to a person I hardly knew. There was no love, no tenderness—just his physical impulses and my longing to be held.

But I soon realized that this non-love-making was not the answer. It only left me feeling used and tossed aside. When I eagerly returned to my marriage commitment, I hoped our occasional opportunities to be together would bring us another child. Susan was two years old and I had a gnawing, unexpressed fear that she would be left an only child, as I had been an only daughter.

While our separate, unshared stresses mounted, my sense of helplessness sometimes pushed me to anger. Susan was subject to severe bouts of tonsillitis and one morning she awoke crying, with an extremely high temperature. Although my anxiety for her approached panic, Jerry apparently was concerned only about his next trucking haul, and our eternal need for money. He was leaving that morning and the car needed repairs, so I would have no transportation to take Susan to the doctor.

Thoroughly frightened for her, I stormed defiantly, "If you leave us now—with Susan this sick—we won't be here when you get back!"

"Where do you think you're going, and how?" he laughed. "You don't have a car. You don't have any money. You can't work and take care of her. You'll be here when I get back!"

He was right, of course, and I was furious. How scared I was! How I hated my lack of independence and inability to take her to the doctor myself. After he left I sponged her continually until her temperature came down.

Eventually I found someone to take us to the doctor, but it was a frightening day, and left me deeply apprehensive about our future.

Compounding my fears was Dad's increasing hostility toward Jerry, which he made no effort to conceal when Jerry was away. It was becoming impossible to defend him, although I still tried. I felt deserted, but trapped—alone, but not free, and I didn't know how to change things.

My second pregnancy did that for me. With wartime gas rationing in effect, I couldn't stay where we were living. We arranged for me and Susan to return to Sonoma County and stay with the Johnsons (who had come out from Illinois with my family eight years before). They had left the Ranch by then and lived in Sonoma, within walking distance to the doctor, which was essential. With all their boys in the service, they had room for us and Jerry agreed to pay for our room and board. He kept his agreement, but we saw very little of him from then on.

This pregnancy was much easier than the first, although it signalled the ultimate separation from Jerry. As the war continued, he served with the Army in Europe, but the break began to seem inevitable before then, while I awaited our second child.

One day during this period I heard from Marty, by then a graduate of the University of California at Berkeley. His letter implied understanding and support, laced with concern. And he asked to see me.

"You always said you could tell me anything," he wrote. "Well, I'm still here for you."

Reading his letter flashed a replay of that morning at high school when I told him we had to part. It was like seeing our ghosts huddled in the corner of the hall—trying to comfort each other—as our puzzled friends passed by on their way to class.

But as I read on, I felt terribly vulnerable—so unsure of everything—and afraid that I couldn't handle seeing him again—couldn't risk rekindling my feelings. I also thought that it would be disloyal to Jerry, so I answered in appreciation, but declined the meeting.

Susan and I moved back to the Ranch shortly before the baby was born. She was three; I was huge and counting the days. Despite Scopalomine and forceps, Karin arrived with less difficulty than Susan, although again I missed being aware for her birth. I was pleased that my little girls would have the sister I had never had and gave Susan, who was eager to "help," every opportunity to assist with the baby's care.

One day while Karin slept in her bassinet on the porch, Susan and I went to check on her and I saw a chair had been placed beside it. Then I noticed that Karin was sleeping on her other side.

"Susan, did you do this?" I asked, as I replaced the chair.

"Karin was fussing, Mommy," she answered matter-of-factly. "I pushed the chair over so I could reach her, and turned her over. I patted her awhile and she went back to sleep."

It didn't occur to her to tell me Karin was fretful, since she felt perfectly capable of taking care of her and loved to do it. Although I had to be watchful of Susan's ingenuity (if the chair had over-balanced the bassinet would have tipped over), I rejoiced in her enjoyment of her little sister. They seemed to be off to a fine beginning together.

Differences in Susan's and Karin's personalities were obvious to us soon after Karin was born. Susan had always been an explorer, seemed totally without fear and began tempting danger before she could walk. Karin was an active baby too, but was much more cautious when she began to navigate. Later on when I took them for rides to new places, Karin would ask, "Mommy, are you sure you know the way home?" And Susan would implore, "Oh Mom, let's get lost today. It would be more fun!"

The years that followed Karin's birth were filled with the care of these two little girls, and the struggle to find a way to support us all. Many have trod this lonely, frightening path and the details of my various decisions, moves, and set-backs are probably similar to those of my single parent "sisters." As our financial and marital situation deteriorated, I couldn't avoid returning to the Ranch periodically for assistance, and greatly appreciated the welcome my parents always gave us.

Six years after Jerry and I were married, I filed for divorce—shuddering over having to charge "cruelty"* as a cause—believing that the real cause was that we were both too young when we started out together.

Susan was deeply and visibly distressed. She loved her daddy and always hoped he would come home to stay—first from his hauling trips, then from the War. Karin had never lived with him and was not fully aware of the situation, but their fatherless childhood severely affected both children.

Mother and Dad seemed eager to help me overcome the difficult beginning of my adult life. I'm sure they wondered if the incest had led to the unmarried pregnancy; I know Mother never stopped wondering.

*In 1945, insufficient support was "mental cruelty" under California law.

I'm also certain that Dad never forgot what he had done, and never acknowledged that it was wrong. He chose instead to assist me. It didn't occur to me then that he was also buying my loyalty.

Because Dad's assistance during and after the end of my marriage seemed supportive of my own efforts—never instead of them— it meant a great deal to me. At the same time, it covered over the unspeakable; like frosting that covers over a crumbling cake and appears to hold it together.

11

SINGLE MOTHER

Santa Barbara 1945-50

There are many remnants of the confusing relationship I had with my father. Throughout my earlier years Dad had engaged in sex talks with me when we were alone, but after I had married, had two children, and was divorced, I thought he had finally given up trying to "educate" me. I was wrong. He was just waiting for a "safe" opportunity. Although unaware of that possibility, but with a strong desire to make an independent life for the three of us, I decided to put some distance between me and my parents. So I moved to Santa Barbara and visited the Ranch for holidays.

When I was twenty-six and the girls (ages six and three), were spending the summer with my parents, I joined them there in August for my two-week vacation. While Mother cared for them on the Ranch, Dad and I took sleeping bags and headed north to the redwood groves. I looked forward to this few days of camping; it was to be my only "break" from a full-time job and child care that I would have that entire year.

During the first afternoon, we set up camp in Stevens Grove and carefully prepared the leaves and redwood needles under our sleeping bags—placed some distance apart. That evening, after a hearty supper cooked over coals, we joined other campers and a ranger for stories and songs around the campfire.

I met a quiet, friendly young man and we began to talk. It was a treat to visit with someone my age in safe, peaceful, natural surroundings. Recently divorced, I was not interested in a serious relationship, but Dad thought otherwise.

Without warning, he said it was time for us to "turn in" and abruptly took me away from the campfire. As we walked through the woods he said, "I don't want him to get any ideas about you." What a disappointment! I was so starved for the casual sociability we were leaving behind. With his words, the first fingers of dread touched the nape of my neck and my head dropped down as I followed him back along the trail.

When we reached our isolated, pitch-dark campsite, he lit the Coleman lantern; but the white light wasn't cheery and the trees were dense and silent. As he dug into his duffel bag and brought out a tablet and pencil, he said, "Why don't you find a book to read? In a few minutes I'll have something to show you." Then he sat down at the picnic table near the lantern. I found a stump in the shadows to sit on and wait—shivering from the cold hand of fear reaching down inside.

He quickly became absorbed and seemed removed from our campsite—smiling as he worked—oblivious to my presence. He didn't look up until he had finished. When he finally called me over, I saw the old glitter in his eyes.

"Come here, Babs, I want you to see this."

As I approached him I felt myself separate in preparation to endure the next unknown. Then I was seated beside him. He put the drawing in front of me—a larger than life picture of female genitalia. As he pointed out the parts, he asked me if Jerry had known how to arouse and satisfy me. I felt suffocated and couldn't answer. My eyes snapped shut in humiliation and shock. I squeezed them tighter to close it all out—silently screaming—

How could he do this!? But he is doing it and I can't find my voice.

While he thoroughly questioned me about the sexual aspects of my failed marriage, he insisted that I look at his drawing with him. Fully clothed, I felt naked and in despair. I behaved exactly as I had as a child: inwardly dismayed and defiled, outwardly passive and compliant.

I still didn't know how to protect myself against him. I didn't know how to shift his focus, and feared that he would ridicule any honest response I might have made. It never occurred to me to confront him—make a demand for propriety, for a change in his attitude toward me.

He finally tired of his perverted inquisition that night and concluded with his old reminder that he was a "very sexy guy." I slid into my sleeping bag and wished I was back in Santa Barbara. Because he hadn't touched me since I was a child, I didn't fear him further and he left me alone.

The pediatrician I worked for in Santa Barbara had recently relocated from the Bay Area and was building up a new practice. So before his days (and mine) became busy we had time to become well-acquainted, while he taught me how to assist him with his young patients. Susan and Karin thought of him as their own doctor and enjoyed coming to the office. His calm, genial manner allayed their fears about "shots" and they loved to joke with him. I felt I had found my niche and life was looking up.

Some months later when he proposed marriage, I delightedly accepted. It felt like a perfectly wonderful idea for all of us. But I was surprised when he said that our engagement should not be announced yet. He said it would not be in his best professional interest while I was still his employee. However, he continued to praise my work, appreciated the extra time I gave on occasion and didn't seem to be in any hurry to set a date for our wedding. Meanwhile, he was eager to establish sexual intimacies as though we were already married; and I believed it was only a matter of time so I complied.

When he continued to attend social affairs at which some of my relatives were present, I was never included. I didn't care for cocktail parties, and probably wouldn't have gone, but I felt unconsidered and unworthy. Although I enjoyed my job, it was becoming increasingly uncomfortable to be the employee, not the wife, of the man I thought I loved.

Our engagement, supposedly secret, was revealed to our parents and mine were happy to meet him. They were very pleased that I would marry a professional man. His mother and sister seemed to welcome the idea as well, and were warm and friendly to me. (His father was deceased.) The fact that he was many years my senior seemed unimportant to any of us; the fact that he had an alcohol problem I felt need not concern anyone either, so didn't tell my family about it. He was great with the children; I enjoyed his company, and he was a considerate employer.

But with failed marriages behind both of us, I was concerned that nothing should spoil this one, especially fears from the past, and I was often haunted by childhood memories of being molested. I still could not believe that Dad was wrong, but I was beginning to wonder— especially after the camping trip.

Thinking he might have been wrong was not enough. I wanted to be *told* that he was, and that I was not crazy for feeling mixed up about it.

One evening I finally found the courage to tell my fiance and ask whether he, as a physician, thought it was important enough for me to worry about, or "should I just try to forget it?" His shocked expression became a distant mask as he responded, "I think what you let your dad do increased your curiosity about sex and is probably why you got pregnant before you were married. You really should have stopped him." My father's responsibility for *his* behavior was not even mentioned, nor did this doctor express any understanding or compassion for me. I felt his disgust, and wished I hadn't broken my silence.

Soon afterwards the axe fell and I was devastated. I lost my temper one day with the girls and shouted at them, not realizing that he could tolerate their misbehavior far better than he could my unexpected explosion. I was not only embarrassed by what I had done, but surprised by his lack of support when the girls clearly needed (and expected) correction in some form. Instead, he broke the engagement and I felt destroyed.

Now I believe that my revelation about the incest was the real reason for his termination of our engagement, such as it was. I believe that his rejection stemmed from revulsion of the known—incest—combined with his fear of the unknown. Was I a mixed-up female who might disgrace him and adversely affect his medical practice?

I kept working for him for almost three more years. Eventually I realized that we wouldn't have been happy for reasons other than my own failings, but I wished I had been aware of them sooner and ended the engagement myself. *I simply could not see flaws in any man on whom I became emotionally dependent.* Dad's "education" was successful in this regard.

During the winter when Karin was six and in the first grade, she became very ill with virus pneumonia, followed by a hemolytic streptococcus infection. It required, in addition to routine blood tests, a long period of rest at home. Since I was working full time, I could not provide the home care she needed.

On their invitation, I took her up north to stay with my parents—under the care of our family physician. Mother assisted her with her lessons and sent regular reports on her progress. As she became stronger, Dad took her with him while he worked around the Ranch or made trips to the valley for supplies. They wrote of the pleasure in having her there to share a lovely spring. I'll always remember Mother's description of Karin's fascination with the California poppies, and the way their little caps popped off as they bloomed.

I have another touching memory of that period. While Susan and I both missed Karin, Susan found a creative way to express it. The girls had twin dolls and using hers as a model, Susan (then nine) skillfully cut out and sewed a beautiful pink, lace-trimmed pinafore for Karin's doll, which she sent her. Susan expressed herself best by undertaking difficult projects and carrying them through. This little dress was an example of that, as well as a gift for her sister.

Fall 1950

After four years, I felt secure in my job and believed I had overcome my sense of personal rejection, but I couldn't avoid feeling discouraged about our future. There would never be an opportunity for me to improve our situation without more formal education, and returning to college at that time was out of the question.

Eventually, the pressures of the situation caught up with me. I developed a recurring, debilitating, elevated temperature which resembled influenza, but was apparently not communicable. An emerging sense that hope was disappearing made my body a perfect target for this strange attack. My body was telling me to seek another direction, while my will was holding on course, afraid of any pause that might lead to total derailment.

I finally took a leave of absence and returned to the Ranch for a rest. The illness recurred periodically for several months before disappearing, but I realized I couldn't return to the overloaded situation that had brought it on. I resigned my job and tried to figure out what to do next. It was validating to learn later that two full-time employees had been hired to take my place.

I do not recall seven-year-old Karin's reaction to our leaving Santa Barbara permanently and returning to the Ranch. She seemed happy to have me with her and she promptly made new friends at school. Ten-year-old Susan, however, resisted the move with acute, vociferous distress that was severe and long-lasting. It engendered a deep rebellion that I believe unfortunately affected the course of her life. At the time I was profoundly concerned, but felt we had no other option.

After we'd been home for several months Kurt, my friend from Illinois and the early days at the Ranch, returned with his children for a visit. It was wonderful to see him again. My girls were delighted with his little boy Jeff and baby girl Karla, whose mother had died the previous year.

Because our families had remained good friends and had kept in touch through the years, Kurt and I felt we knew each other very well— possibly better than we knew anyone else. We spent several nights before the living room fire, catching up on our recent lives and talking into the early morning. We felt warm and affectionate, but not passionate, which seemed comfortable under the circumstances. My parents and our children were sleeping nearby.

In recalling our personal relationship as teenagers we realized we had become a mix of pals, siblings, and occasional antagonists. Kurt had expressed regret when I announced my marriage to Jerry saying, "I had always hoped to marry you myself some day." It was the first indication he had given about his feelings for me; expressed too late for me to even consider.

As we shared the changes that had occurred since then, it was inevitable for us to discuss marriage. Since I had re-buried my primary anxiety about incest, I addressed another doubt I had concerning my role as a wife and parent.

"There's one thing that worries me, Kurt, because it may bother you and I can't promise that I can change."

"What could that be? I'm sure I won't be bothered," he responded with an amused grin.

He has never taken my concerns seriously, so I guess it may not be very important, but I have to tell him anyway—

"You know, I've been alone with Susan and Karin for over seven years—making all the decisions for us. I feel a little mixed about sharing responsibility for them now. It's strange, I long to have someone who cares about us to talk things over with, but if we didn't agree about them, I'm afraid I wouldn't want to compromise. I don't think you'd like that."

"I know we'll do just fine," he said. "Don't worry about it because I'm not." And that disposed of my only expressed concern.

Although I knew Kurt cared for me, he had usually shown it in amusing, non-serious gestures and although I had confided in him through the years, I had never told him about Dad. I wasn't remotely aware of our deeply buried inhibitions to intimacy. Blocking out Dad's abuses, I concentrated on those characteristics of his that I valued and extended some of them to Kurt. Both men shared a love for country living, non-material values and willingness to share household chores and the obvious responsibilities of a family. These were the qualities of a dependable mate that I had been missing. Underneath it all I was really searching for the trustworthy, non-sexually aggressive father I had never had. I longed to transcend my sense of shame and in matching Kurt's dispassionate approach I hoped to earn his respect.

I trusted Kurt and was certain our long friendship was the best possible beginning for us, so we decided to get married. Reactions to our decision were varied. Our children were pleased, as they looked forward to happier times. Our parents and their friends seemed over-joyed (and were probably relieved). But some of our peers were surprised because, as one of them said later, "You always seemed like brother and sister." At the time, though, this didn't occur to us.

Our wedding brought the two families together after a number of turbulent years, following the five years they had shared on the Ranch. We chose a garden setting. Under a canopy of oaks beside the pool graced with water lilies, Dad had planted blue delphiniums to match my dress. They were all in bloom.

Jeff in a crisp white suit, and the girls in pink dresses with flowers in their hair, enthusiastically participated in the ceremony, giving us all a sense of family. One of my fondest memories is of a beaming Karin and her new little brother Jeff dancing together.

When Kurt and I returned from our honeymoon, we quickly set aside our newly-wed role to resume parenting. But I immediately sensed an arcane cloud hovering over us that made me uneasy. I felt Dad's lack of warmth toward Kurt's children and noted his jokes at their expense. In light of the changes in their young lives this seemed cruel. It disturbed me. But true to form, I couldn't confront him and speak up for them. Kurt did not seem to notice it.

Later that afternoon I carried little Karla down the path and into the redwoods—my sanctuary—where I held her for a quiet moment and promised aloud to take good care of her. She understood my tone and hug, if not my words, and softly patted my cheek. I wish I'd been able to keep that promise.

12

FIRST GLIMPSE
OF THE LEGACY

There were difficult facts about their lives that Kurt's two children eventually had to know. He had been married twice before he married me in 1951. His first marriage brought him a son, Jeff, but ended in divorce, with Kurt obtaining custody of his baby boy. His second marriage gave Jeff a new mother and then a sister, but this second wife died when Karla was fifteen months old and Jeff was under five years. My girls had always known about this, but because Jeff continued to grieve for the only mother he could remember, and Karla didn't remember living with anyone but us, we hadn't felt any urgency about telling them.

One day while Kurt was at work the two children were talking on the back steps. They were just below the open kitchen window, where I was preparing vegetables at the sink. When Jeff's voice reached me I was startled to hear him ask Karla, "D'you know why I get mad at Mom sometimes?"

"No—why?"

"Because she's not my real mom. You didn't know that, did you?"

"You're foolin' me, Jeff. Why do you say that?"

"Because it's true. My real mom died when you were a baby."

"Now I know you're just pretending. Nobody really died."

Before he could tell her that I wasn't *her* mother either, I dried my hands and quickly joined them outside. I had always pictured their father would be the one to tell them. But the time had arrived and couldn't be postponed, without destroying the open atmosphere I hoped would make it easier for them.

It was a poignant, utterly sad moment. I told Jeff that the mother he still loved was not his first mother, but that she had loved him as her own little boy. Then I told Karla that I was not her first mother either. I tried to be gentle, but it felt awful to see their shock and incredulous expressions. They must have cried many times afterwards for those first mothers they couldn't remember, but if they did, I never knew it.

I feel very sad about Jeff's boyhood. I wanted to be what he needed, but I wasn't. I didn't know how. I felt his resentment about my marriage to his dad, but was unable to acknowledge it with him, so that we could go on from there.

One time Jeff found a box of Kurt's letters written to me before our marriage. When I discovered him reading them I was furious and made a scene. My feelings were straight out of my own childhood when Mother read my letters. I assumed Jeff was looking for love-words between Kurt and me with a curiosity similar to Mother's. Wrong! I still remember the stab of remorse I felt when he stopped crying long enough to sob, "I just wanted to know if Dad wrote anything about *me*."

I wanted to be a good mother to all of them, but I don't believe they always felt that I loved them. We had many trying times while everyone was growing up, and because our sense of emotional security was so thin, with big rips all through it, we sometimes failed to "be there" for each other, no matter how hard we tried.

Some of the children developed unusual behavior patterns, such as sleep-walking and bed-wetting, that hadn't been a problem at first. I knew they were symptoms of inner stress, but assumed they stemmed from the expanded family situation and hoped they would outgrow them.

Many youngsters pass through stages when their language is almost unintelligible; they apparently understand each other, but their mumbling and sawed-off words are an annoying mystery to their parents. Karin and Jeff both went through this phase, although Karin's was much more pronounced than Jeff's. She appeared unable to open her mouth. Her jaw was tensely locked and almost shut when she spoke. Since this developed in an otherwise healthy child and she did not complain of pain, I thought it best to ignore it and hoped it would subside. But it didn't and I didn't recognize it as a symptom that would gain chilling significance in hindsight.

In April, 1953 Beth was born. During the ten years since Karin's birth, many changes had developed in physicians' attitudes toward the process of childbirth. I welcomed each one.

Although Kurt was not permitted in the delivery room, my doctor readily complied with my insistence that Scopalomine be avoided, so I was awake, aware and able to be helpful. The doctor in praising me said, "You just handed her to me." Then I topped it all off by walking from the delivery room to my bed in the maternity section—on the doctor's arm. I felt fully redeemed as an adequate woman, able to have babies normally.

The next day while I was preparing to take a shower, the Catholic nurse-sister in her flowing white habit came in to instruct me. First she warned me not to use a washcloth between my legs. She matter-of-factly said to wash myself with my hands, because there would be much less chance of infection than if I used the cloth. I could not believe my ears. Although I said nothing, my round eyes must have communicated surprise; but she went on advising about the care of my breasts, and other matters of personal hygiene. I felt as though I had just been given permission by God to treat my whole body as though it belonged to me. I was thirty-two years old.

There was another reward for my persistence and medicine's advancement back to "basics." I was able to nurse this baby for seven months. She never had a bottle at all—just went from me to a cup. What a blessing—especially on the camping trips that we enjoyed with the older children.

Beth seldom cried. When I checked to see if she was awake, hungry, or needed changing, she would often be serenely smiling, cooing to herself, alert and comfortable. I usually had to awaken her in the morning for her first feeding. During the summer I'd take her to the swimming pool where she "breakfasted" while the older children had their Red Cross swimming lessons.

One morning Dad dropped by. I called to him from our bedroom, where I was bathing Beth. In the corner we had a large, high table, covered with oilcloth that I dressed and bathed her on. She was a few months old—calm and relaxed in the basin of water—even when I washed her face. I was enjoying this pleasant interlude in a busy day, and when Dad came in he watched her a few minutes, then joined my mood, saying, "Isn't she a sweet little thing? What a happy, contented baby." I basked in motherly pride and agreement.

Our conversation drifted to her not having been a boy, when I heard him say, *"You can never bring me too many little girls."* The words stabbed like a knife thrust deep into my gut! They jerked me away from the innocent present, and back into our murky past. I never wanted to be reminded of his molesting me, and yet it happened so suddenly, I couldn't ignore it.

Although I continued smiling and pretending that everything was still the same in our little baby-bathing scene, it wasn't. Thoughts of my daughters being touched as I had been assailed me unbidden. I tried to put them off as being paranoid.

*After all, he wouldn't think of overstepping the bounds
again—would he?*

I hated the question! It had never surfaced before and I couldn't chase it away with any rationalizing thought I might cling to, in an effort to erase those fears. I hated the question because I couldn't answer it, and I couldn't conceive of confronting him. He remained in control of our times together—I was powerless and passive, as usual.

Rachel, our sixth child, was born when Beth was twenty months old and we decided that our family was now complete. Once again, I walked out of the delivery room, and went on to nurse Rachel for eleven months.

Because I knew how lonely it felt, I empathized with Jeff's position as our only boy. I was sorry that he would not have a little brother, but was happy that our two youngest daughters would have each other.

Rachel was much livelier than Beth—especially at night when she liked to entertain. But although she, too, cried very little, she was highly stimulated by her surroundings and responsive to them. There was no nursing at the swimming pool with her; we had to be quietly by ourselves for her to calmly complete her meal.

One of my characteristic behavior patterns during those years was a sudden negative response to interruptions, due to my compulsion to set a tight course through the day's activities. With small children, interruptions form a major part of one's life and even though I knew this, I handled them erratically. I hated my unpredictable eruptions that hurt those I loved. I wanted so much to have them respect and trust me, but they couldn't when my behavior made them feel insecure and unsure of me.

I did try to answer their rare questions about sex, despite a sarcastic voice inside that taunted: "You phoney—you really don't know what you're talking about." It was hard to ignore this inner scorn while doggedly carrying on the discussion. Although I was eager to establish healthy sexual attitudes, I was determined not to badger them as Mother had done to me, so I didn't question them, and probably avoided raising the issue in ways that could have been helpful.

Not long ago one of my daughters said, "I always thought of you as a good mother. You seemed to know how to parent. I felt you understood children well and enjoyed being with them."

After years of self-doubts this was music to my ears.

Then she asked, "Because you were sexually abused as a child, did you ever think of sexually abusing any of us?"

Her question surprised me—such a possibility had never occurred to me. And that's just what I told her—glad that she had the courage to ask me. It's so awful to harbor sexual doubts about a parent.

In May 1955, when Rachel was four months old, my father died. Following an automobile accident the previous year, his health had deteriorated and he was hospitalized with various acute conditions from then on. Bedridden for some time before he died, his death released him from months of pain. I refused to view his body afterward, saying I preferred to remember him as he used to be—healthy and happy on the Ranch.

Susan turned fifteen the day after Dad died and Karin was almost twelve. In a misguided effort to spare them further grief, I kept them away from his funeral. In so doing, I unwittingly sabotaged the normal grieving process that leads to acceptance, and distanced us even further from awareness of the hidden truth about him.

But there were circumstances in which my highly developed denial system did not operate, which allowed my responses to be in line with reality. For example, when Jeff, not yet six, told us that an adult friend of our relatives had exposed himself to Jeff and engaged him in fondling, we believed him and I was furious. I reassured Jeff that he was right to tell us and that he would never have to see that man again. We told the relatives, as a warning for their own children.

Later we were informed that when they asked their friend about it he denied everything, then ran to the bathroom and vomited—saying he was deeply hurt over our accusations. This happened more than thirty years before sexual abuse of children was discussed as openly as it is today, and I felt doubly angry that Jeff was not believed. We all knew that a five-year-old boy didn't know enough to make up a story like that. But at least Jeff knew that Kurt and I believed him. None of us ever saw that man again.

As time went on I began to feel that my life wasn't normal, and that I couldn't provide a normal life for my family. Unwanted reminders of abusive sexual activity began to confront me when I least expected it. In fact, incest continued to intrude as it always had—on the simplest scenes—on everything. It was slowly poisoning our family life as it touched each one.

A few years after the abuse of Jeff by someone we hardly knew, I found myself unable to cope in that same straightforward manner when Susan came to me one morning in a rage. I was in the kitchen, kneading bread.

"Mom, I want to talk to you—in your room," she stormed. She rushed me to the bedroom and slammed the door.

Unable to contain herself another minute, she cried out, "Do you know what's happened to Karla?" I didn't know that anything had happened to her, but Susan didn't wait for an answer.

"She just told me that when she went fishing with Uncle Lee, he messed around with her. He made her fondle him. Mom—he was awful!"

Spinning—falling—trying to surface—

"He did?" I heard myself say in a faint, far-away voice that made Susan even more irate.

"Mom, you have to DO something—NOW! What's the matter with you?"

"I don't know. I can't think."

Like trying to run in a dream—I'm frozen—can't move—can't answer—

Susan gave up on me and flung herself out of the room.

For uncounted minutes I sat there and tried to work through the clouds of numbness in my head, but I couldn't feel any anger, or find any words, or conceive any idea about what I should do. Unlike Jeff's abuser, Lee is my brother. Something had clicked inside when Susan told me about what he had done—leaving me confused and incapacitated.

I knew Susan spoke the truth. In a hidden recess of my mind, I knew Lee was capable. The revolting memory of his frequently exposed genitals, as he sprawled awkwardly in a living room chair, flashed before me. And I hated his smirk of pretended oblivion to our feelings.

No one had said a word to him when he did this, although small, puzzled children were present. We merely turned away—trying not to see—until he repositioned himself. His smirk was not the brazen leer that made eye contact, like my dad's—but a smutty, inner grin to himself. I had no way of knowing then that Dad's leer spawned Lee's smirk and that both came from the same predatory urge.

I could hear the children's voices outside, but felt disconnected from everything. Homemade bread—our "staff of life"—could not begin to meet Karla's needs. Suddenly our wholesome values and country surroundings seemed flimsy and irrelevant. They couldn't counteract the unseen poison.

In the days that followed, although I wanted to reassure Susan, I couldn't bring myself to talk to Karla about Lee—a member of my own family. Shame was in control. I felt I had broken the pledge I made to her when I first became her mother—to take good care of her. And I was locked inside the old unspoken incest command: Don't acknowledge it, you'll just make it more real.

So all I did afterward was to see that none of the children was alone with Lee again; no more invitations to join us on camping trips, during which it was easy to go off fishing; no more hikes up Graham Canyon when we were visiting the Ranch; all of which he had done with various ones of them through the years. But I couldn't allow myself to wonder if Karla had been his only victim.

My feelings finally came up when I told Kurt about it and to my distress he remained unperturbed. If he felt fatherly rage he didn't show it. He, too, made no move to confront Lee.

However, his non-reaction was typical for him, since he always minimized emotionally-charged or sexual problems, especially when I was upset. Years later I realized that the rebuke, "If you're not part of the solution, you're part of the problem," applied to him. For by then I knew he was deeply conflicted about sex himself and the familiar reproof foreshadowed offenses far in the future.

But at the time, all I knew was that without Kurt's active support, I had to "stuff my feelings" when I was around Lee, just as I had as a child around Dad.

I knew Lee would get away with furious denials if I confronted him by myself and that Karla would be accused of lying, as Jeff had been. I felt I had to protect her from that form of further destructive abuse. So, aside from not allowing the children to be alone with him, I tried to act as though nothing had happened. He was as safe from my suppressed rage, and his exposure, as our father before him had been. And their evil legacy thrived on undisturbed.

13

REACHING OUT

1959

Automatically, like the little girl who had shoved down her fears about her father and tried to forget what he did to her, I shoved down my anger about my brother and couldn't see the connection.

But I longed to find acceptable expression for my strong, bewildering, misunderstood emotions that too often ran away with me. I longed for a sense of balance in my life—a sense of self respect that continued to elude me, no matter how hard I worked. Perhaps, I thought, I should reach out beyond my focus here at home. So I began to go to church regularly—a conventional, tentative and safe first step.

Through the older children's participation in the youth groups, Kurt and I eventually joined the Methodist Church. I became interested in peace and civil rights issues while discussing them with members of the social concerns committee. As I learned more, I sensed a growing rebellion against injustice and against those institutions and persons that had abused their power. I identified with underdogs and embraced their causes, unaware that I was using their battles to fight my own.

Of course I drew fire, but I was never alone. There were others—experienced with non-violent protest—for me to turn to. I felt a network of support in and out of the church and it felt good. I wrote, marched, sang, included my family in San Francisco peace marches, NAACP functions, and explored issues with them. I made friends along the way and felt as though we belonged to something important beyond ourselves.

As a family we observed the various farm workers' boycotts and hoped that conditions for them would improve. When Cesar Chavez invited our church group to join them as they marched from Delano to Sacramento, I walked with them from Stockton to Lodi on my day off from a full time job. I felt privileged to be asked and wouldn't have missed it.

For several years, two young black women from Kenya lived with us while attending college—bringing a new dimension to our awareness of the world and the people in it.

During the early 60s I wrote a letter to church leaders urging them to consider racial integration of the pulpits. A copy was given to the Rev. Cecil Williams (a black Methodist minister in San Francisco), who then wanted to discuss it with me.

If my premise seemed naive, he was courteous enough not to show it. Instead, he seemed surprised about the depth of my concerns, how far I had ventured in expressing them, and was willing to help take my challenge further. As we talked he asked me, "Where did this come from; what turned you on to this?" I had absolutely no answer then, or for many years thereafter.

I was also trying to live up to the super-mom role at home and taxiing the children to everything, since we lived four miles out of town. Kurt valiantly tried to keep up with it all. If our personal communication was limited, we were so busy we didn't notice—at least not at first.

Although we had been friends for eighteen years before we married, in truth I did not know him very well. But the years growing up together had given us both the feeling that we shared an intuitive understanding, which we viewed as an unusual and important bond. I remember Kurt saying to my parents when we told them of our decision to marry, "We are so in tune that we often know what the other one is going to say before we say it."

During the early years of our marriage, we confidently built on our mutual interests and values, without realizing that along the way we were not expressing our desires, doubts and differences. Kurt had always seemed strong and able to control his emotions—a quality that I greatly admired when we were teenagers. When I observed his coolness then, it made me feel safer from my own emotions and I tried to emulate his self control.

But as time went on, this coolness began to feel like distance and it made me uneasy. I yearned to be affectionately held or fondly touched, but didn't know how to tell him this. We had slowly allowed the bond we cherished for its intuitive quality to become a barrier against open, candid discussions. Eventually, the bond became bondage and estranged us from each other.

For me, who had always felt estranged from my family, it was an extension of the alienation I'd always known, and it frightened me. My

sense of being flawed moved me farther and farther away from acknowledging a problem that I couldn't understand.

After six years we began life apart under the same roof. Although
we gave Kurt's tendency to snore as the reason for our new arrangement, I felt that both of us used that as an excuse. We didn't really want
to continue sharing a bed. When we occasionally spent part of a night
together, we felt more like kind friends being nice to each other than
lovers.

I hoped that the long lapses between intercourse (often six
months), would rekindle my own responses. But even when I initiated
sex, I could never break through the passivity that then overtook me.
I felt apart—from him and from my self. For years I thought my
numbness was denying us both fulfillment. I didn't realize that he, too,
lacked access to his feelings.

Gradually I discovered that Kurt's quiet demeanor did not always
reflect inner calm. It sometimes held down deep anger and hostility.
Tensions between us began to mount and during the twelfth year of our
marriage it felt as though we went from one downward slide to another.

One of my worst memories follows the day I had two wisdom
teeth removed from the right side of my jaw. That evening the pain
medication was insufficient and, since we couldn't reach the dentist, we
went to the hospital emergency room. There I was given something
stronger, but by the time we came home, two hours later, I was
exhausted.

In the meantime, one of the girls had become extremely upset. As
we came in, she was unaware of my frazzled state and focused her
outbursts on me. I responded angrily and then fell apart. My last shreds
of control scattered as I retreated to my room, crying hysterically.

Kurt quickly followed. With his huge hand he slapped my face
hard, several times. The sudden intense pain wiped out whatever
adrenalin was feeding my hysteria. But I immediately felt dead—
drained of even a spark of life or hope. Kurt glared at me with eyes like
cold steel and didn't say a word. I felt his total power. I thought,

His love for me must be gone, for him to have hit me
so hard.

There was no one there to stop him—only (as I learned years
later), frightened young children in their beds, whose world was falling
apart.

The next day the entire left side of my face was black and blue and
my eye was swollen closed. I had a routine doctor's appointment that

day, and he looked at me in disbelief when I told him about the difficult extraction of my teeth.

"But they were on the other side," he reminded me.

When I couldn't bring myself to tell him more, the doctor quietly looked me in my good right eye and said, "You're too nice to have something like that happen to you."

Even though I knew that he knew, I just tucked his kind words away inside, not to be believed for years, but never forgotten.

Our household was rapidly shrinking as Susan, Karin and Jeff left to pursue their own lives. Kurt and I began to drift blindly and felt ourselves floundering. I tried not to notice his coolness and thought we just missed the pleasures we had shared before when the children were younger and all still at home. But life had become tasteless. It seemed to contain more work and struggle than meaning and joy.

By this time I had been working in the office of the children's school for five years. When that job ended, I found work as a hospital aide. But I began without any nurses training, which would have included precautions against involvement with the personal problems of patients.

As I discovered some of their appalling circumstances, I couldn't ignore my compassion for them and their families. There were young mothers of several small children—dying with cancer; there was a young man paralyzed from a diving accident, another with brain injuries, and a number with slowly healing fractures, who inadvertently revealed other problems in their lives—such as being unable to read and write.

The inevitable question arose in me—how to help them? For most, their problems were beyond my reach, or knowing where to turn. I could only try to be their friend and make them as comfortable as I knew how. But I welcomed the opportunity the job provided to do this much, and to feel better about myself.

Since I was working the evening shift (4 p.m. to 12:30 a.m.), we looked forward to my evenings off and celebrated with special dinners and games—even on school nights. Kurt began to seem more relaxed, the children were intrigued with my new type of work, and we were all in better spirits than we had been for some time.

One evening I was feeling unusually optimistic and close to them. The conversation at dinner had been sprinkled with jokes and light-hearted conversation, as we exchanged happenings at school and on our jobs.

Later that evening, Kurt and I relaxed in front of the fire. It felt good to be with him, watching the embers die down, in almost the same sense of quiet companionship we had felt so many years before. The children had gone to bed.

When I invited him to join me while we prepared for bed ourselves, his smile quickly disappeared; replaced by his drawn, uncomfortable look I had come to dread in the past.

His eyes slid away from mine, "No, Barb, I don't believe I want to."

Sudden knot forming in my stomach—What have I done?

"Oh, I guess I shouldn't have asked, but you seemed so happy tonight. And it's been such a long time."

"I know it has," he replied, "but I've wanted to tell you. I don't want us to have relations anymore."

CRASH! I don't need to ask him why—I know he's stopped loving me—Now I wish I hadn't suggested it—Just gives him more reason to think I'm too sexy— more reason not to respect me—more reason to feel superior because he doesn't want what I know I need. I don't please him—I want to, but I never know how he feels—he doesn't tell me. Now I'll never know because it's over. Ohhh—I don't want it to be over— even if I never feel blended with him—even if there are months between—there was always a hope—now there's nothing!

I smiled weakly in embarrassment as we moved away from the dark fireplace, toward our separate rooms.

Had I brought this upon myself in reaching out beyond our home? Did Kurt feel abandoned as my interests expanded? But it was too late to turn away from them now. Each one had helped us all to grow.

I felt pulled both ways. I knew that the sexual failure with Kurt would always tarnish any outside satisfactions, as the sense of being dirty with my dad when I was young had tarnished my accomplishments at school. My childhood feeling of being two persons was returning. Lying awake and alone at night I was afraid.

With his decision to shut the door between us permanently, I believed that achieving closeness and sexual pleasure was a lost cause for me. I was forty-six years old.

14

CAPTIVES

Winter 1966

One Saturday morning after breakfast, we lingered around the kitchen table and looked forward to my first weekend off in quite awhile. As we prepared to tackle the weekly chores, Kurt retreated into his own world and showed no enthusiasm for the family outing we planned for later on. He was so glum, preoccupied and unresponsive, I didn't try to involve him further.

But after the girls began their tasks, I called him aside so I knew we wouldn't be overheard.

"I'm worried, Kurt," I began, "You seem so far away from us. What's the matter?"

His frown of discomfort formed as he answered impatiently, "Oh—come on—I don't know what you mean. I'm fine—a little tired maybe—nothing to worry about. You know, Barb, you're always imagining something."

"I can't help feeling you're unhappy and I'm afraid it's because of me."

Annoyed at my persistence he started to reply, "You're being over-sensitive," but I didn't let him finish. I interrupted (which he hated), and pushed on: "Please—you always say that about me and maybe I am. But I'm also very concerned about *us*. Can't we talk about it?"

Irritated and defensive, he countered, "There's nothing to talk about."

I took the plunge. "Maybe this sounds crazy, but it seems like your feelings for me have changed. Sometimes I wonder if you ever did love me." I rushed on. "Maybe for you, it was just a marriage of convenience," I finally choked out.

Tell me I'm wrong—tell me you really care.

Instead I heard, "What's the matter with a marriage of convenience?"—an admission, not a question. Devastated, I couldn't bring myself to ask,

That's all it was for you?

So that final question hung unanswered in the air.

We left the room—rejoined the children—and I went on pretending. The children reported cheerfully on their chores as they tried to read our faces, and went on pretending, too.

One day someone was admitted to the hospital who behaved so differently from the other patients that I began to feel challenged to help him beyond the usual duties of nursing care. His disruptive manner often ostracized him from the sympathy of the staff and I unconsciously began to identify with Don's feelings of rejection, engendered by his hostile behavior.

Our personal relationship began when he showed me a poem that he had written a few years before—while he was in prison. It was his way of letting me know where he'd been and testing me to see if I would still be his friend. For me, it was a green light. How could I abandon such a lonely outcast and still consider myself compassionate?

Don soon began to confide in me and let me know that he appreciated my care. Although his intense manner was flattering, it sometimes disturbed me, because I wasn't sure of my feelings for him.

By the time he was able to leave the hospital, Kurt had come up to meet him and, since Don had no home to return to, we invited him to stay with us.

It was to be a temporary arrangement. We lived near the hospital and could provide him the transportation that he needed to return for daily out-patient treatments.

Shortly before he was released from the hospital, Don phoned me one day at home to reaffirm his regard for me and his appreciation of our offer. But I felt mixed about the warm tone in his voice, and hoped he wasn't being overheard. While he talked I had a sudden uneasy flash that he might arouse the same confusing feelings in my young daughters—feelings I couldn't deny in myself.

That afternoon when I came on duty I cautiously mentioned my concern.

"You know, Don, you can be quite the charmer, and I hope you'll realize that my girls might not understand if you compliment them the way you do me. They're very young, and you're so different from their dad."

Instantly his expression became stormy. "How could you say that? How could you even think I might lead them on?" He was so hurt and angry I quickly apologized, and firmly disowned the instincts that tried to warn me.

The timing of his coming to our home was perfect—for him. The day that he arrived was the day that Kurt received dreadful news about his job. The department he had worked so hard for sixteen years to build from scratch was being shelved and he was being demoted. He was in shock.

Don, with his uncanny opportunism and quick perception of our areas of vulnerability, stepped in to capitalize on this disaster with amazing skill and ingenuity. Within three months, he had assisted Kurt in buying new clothes, energized his successful search for a new job, and we had a new home. Kurt was even spared the unpleasantness of selling our much-loved Santa Rosa home and arranging for our relocation. Don, the new "family member," engineered the entire operation and we were swept up in his enthusiasm. Somehow leaving Santa Rosa and moving 200 miles north, where we knew no one, was more like an exciting adventure than a sad up-rooting.

We quickly settled into a roomy country home near Lake Shasta, and Kurt began working in Redding—ten miles away. Our drifting was over; purpose had returned to our lives, and we felt that we owed our new sense of hope entirely to Don. He immodestly agreed. To express our gratitude, we encouraged him to stay on while he searched for new direction in his own life.

During that first summer of 1967, we invited Mother for a visit. She lived on the Ranch still, with someone to care for her, having survived heart problems and strokes; but she had refused to give up and remain an invalid. The sharp edges of her tactless comments were gone.

She had planned to stay for a week. When we urged her to stay for two, she was delighted. Then, a few nights after her birthday that fall, celebrated with my brothers in San Francisco, she died quietly in her sleep.

From the beginning two years before, Don had professed a determination to complete his education. He scored high on all the tests he took and enrolled in classes at Shasta College. However, a self-defeating pattern soon emerged. He would attend classes, become acquainted with the instructors, and make a favorable impression. But he would stay just long enough to obtain expensive textbooks, and then drop out. He didn't complete a single course. We were continually having our hopes for him raised with each new semester, only to have them dashed; after which he would disappear for several days.

When our adult children and extended families entertained doubts about Don's motives, Kurt and I shut them out and maintained a closed front where he was concerned. In effect, we provided a perfect cover for the anti-social behavior he'd engaged in since childhood.

Step by step, we were drawn in through his manipulation of the unmet needs of each one of us. When he recognized Kurt's lack of a recreational hobby, he persuaded him to buy a boat, and the two of them fished for many long weekends on Shasta Lake. He discovered my penchant for writing and put me to work on his autobiography, which I transcribed from his tape-recorded memories.

But when alone with this unrecognized sexual abuser, I became like putty in his hands. When he showered me with attention, I couldn't resist his further advances. Since he cast me in the role of a respectably restrained "lady"—above enjoying a passionate affair—my passive response in bed was just what he wanted. I pretended to myself that the numbness wasn't there.

I wanted to say NO, but deeply missed feeling special to someone, and I believed he truly cared for me. As he gained more control over all of us, though, his sexual interest in me waned, and I felt dumped (again). But I was also relieved, and felt cleaner about our relationship.

With each one of the three younger girls Don sought to establish himself as a trusted, loving confidante, as well as the "uncle" who could tell them what to do. Through his demands, they became more adept at cooking and cleaning than I had ever required of them.

I have since learned that teenage Karla, frightened and sexually abused by Lee and others during her childhood, fell under Don's spell and believed that he sincerely returned her love. When she discovered that he was trying to go as far as he could with everyone he knew, her private grief nearly destroyed her.

Insidiously, we all began to fear displeasing him, as every aspect of our lives (including our finances) came under his scrutiny and total control. Kurt had attempted once (during the first summer) to question our drift, but quickly gave up when Don reminded him that our circumstances were better than before we moved north. Kurt's new job, new friends and fishing became his refuge from a situation he didn't like, but didn't know how to change.

Despite Mother's strong admonitions against it years before (or because of them on an unconscious level), I decided to become a licensed vocational nurse. During my training it was easy for me to let Don usurp my parenting responsibilities. I was either bone-tired or studying when I was at home. But I was not aware of the destructive direction that his volatile personality was taking us until it was far too late. When he developed heart problems, his "temporary" stay secured itself even more solidly.

Despite his denials, Don thrived on the edge of disaster, and felt best when he was manipulating others. When he used his ailing heart as a means for control, I became his hostage. I felt compelled to meet his demands, or (he made me believe) risk causing his death.

One summer day while visiting Lake Tahoe we went for a drive, intending to spend the afternoon outdoors. As we were leaving town, a car with four young people in it passed us. I saw nothing wrong with the way the car was being handled, but Don immediately exploded, "Cut in on me, you bastards—I'll show you!" And he speeded up, blew the horn and began to tailgate them.

They were looking back in amazement when Don whipped out a small gun and aimed it at them—through the windshield. The kids faces turned to horror, as I screamed at him to put down the gun. But he didn't. He continued to chase them—swearing all the while—steering with only his left hand—his right hand steadily aiming the gun at the kids in the car ahead of us. We were all in the hands of a maniac out of control.

Suddenly the Highway Patrol office appeared on our left and the kids swerved across the road and rushed in, as we continued out of town. I was terrified and crying; Don was suddenly, completely cool. His rage was gone. He knew exactly what he was going to do next.

We left the main road and took another which led up into the hills. He stopped the car in an isolated spot, where we didn't see any cars or homes at all. Then he got out of the car and threw the gun as far as he could over a steep, densely-treed embankment. After he turned the car around, we drove back toward town. I couldn't believe it.

"They must be looking for us," I said, "Why are we going back?"

"They're not expecting us to be going in this direction," he assured me. And they weren't. As we merged with the incoming traffic on the main road, we heard the sirens approaching ahead of us in the opposite lane. Next, several patrol cars went screaming past and headed out of town without seeing us. I was a wreck—wanting their protection, but afraid to move.

Don hid out in a hotel room and returned home later, while I drove the car back to Redding that night—frightened all the way. I had no idea what I would say if I were stopped. I had seen a side of Don that terrorized and silenced me.

At home, Don's frequent stormy disruptions, night and day, had made his initial role of helping us a faded memory. Increasingly, he would rampage around angered by a variety of imagined slights, then flip-flop back to behaving himself and soliciting our understanding. But Jeff, while visiting for a few days with his wife and baby son, tried to bring us to our senses.

One morning when Kurt was at work, Jeff and I were caught in an argument. Suddenly Don appeared—wildly firing his new gun and scaring us out of our wits. "Get out of the family," he shouted at Jeff. "You don't belong here!"

Still under Don's incredible control, I concurred with his dreadful command to Jeff. In the years since that happened, Jeff has appeared to understand and forgive, but I still don't forgive myself.

Although emotionally and physically exhausted, I somehow completed my nursing course and obtained my license. However, it had become impossible for me to do my best—anywhere. I didn't even know what it would feel like to do my best.

One afternoon, in despair over my sense of entrapment, I angrily accused Don of deliberately stringing everyone along with his outrageous antics. He couldn't bear to have me get so assertive and close to the truth, and became enraged.

"You have no right to criticize me just because I live here," he ranted. "You owe everything to me. I saved all of you from going down the drain in Santa Rosa and without me you'd all be nothing!" His dark eyes flashed hatred as he stormed at me, jabbing his finger in my face and cutting me down with insults.

Suddenly I realized I was dealing with a monster who was driving me crazy. I ran to the bathroom and locked the door. I remember how the sight of my face in the mirror triggered enormous self revulsion. *I* had become the monster and I deeply hated myself more than him or anyone else. With both hands and unmindful of pain, I tried to rip my face off.

My face, my face—that naked part of me I couldn't ever hide.

Don began pounding on the bathroom door and I finally emerged, afraid that if I didn't he would break it down. His response when he saw me was to call the girls upstairs.

"Look what you did to your mother!" he raved, as they stared in horror at my bleeding face. They had done nothing to deserve this accusation, but I couldn't defend them. I felt like a robot—not alive.

Rachel told me years later that they thought I was losing my mind and they were terrified. With the memory still vivid, she said, "I remember seeing your scratched face and blank, beaten expression. I was very scared of Don and tried desperately to cry and feel remorse for something I felt I didn't do—anything to quiet him down. I sensed that you really didn't blame us and were also powerless to say so. I knew I could hold on to my kernel of truth and survive—but I wasn't sure you could."

We were living in chaos, trying to grasp the tiniest corner of reality and hang on.

Inevitably, I made a decision about committing suicide, and it felt good to know that I didn't have to remain trapped indefinitely. When I told Don that my way out would be over Shasta Dam because, "it would leave no mess," he ridiculed me.

"You're just trying to scare me, but I know you don't mean it," he mocked.

That time, he was wrong. I did mean it. And as long as I lived there I felt safer emotionally, knowing I could escape life permanently if ever I couldn't hang on any longer. Irrational as this decision appears in retrospect, at the time I felt greatly relieved after I made it.

When I sensed that we were all being dragged into a bottomless undertow, and I was losing touch with everyone I cared about, I panicked and became less able to cope with it. The common childhood fear/dream of falling into a bottomless pit was becoming real. When I finally woke up, it was the beginning of my long journey to enlightenment.

> "A rule of thumb is,
> The more difficult it is to
> end a relationship that is
> bad for you, the more elements
> of the childhood struggle
> it contains."
>
> Robin Norwood
> **WOMEN WHO LOVE TOO MUCH**

One morning I clearly knew what I had to do and caught Don in mid-storm. Power surged up inside—strong words marched firmly out.

"You have to leave—NOW—and you can never come back."

Then in anticipation of his defense I continued, "I don't care if your heart stops permanently on the front steps—I'm never going to pick you up again!"

He looked stunned. But I ignored his protests—gave him two hours to pack—and felt wonderful. This time he believed me—and left.

Susan also confronted him at about the same time (when I wasn't home), and between the two of us his several attempts to return did not work. He was permanently out of our lives.

It had taken five long years for me to come to my senses. Don left a family in emotional shambles, turned some of us against each other, took us to the brink of financial ruin, exploited each of us in every imaginable way, and brought me years of remorse.

Although we couldn't survive such prolonged agony without learning something about ourselves and the price of misplacing our trust, it was a destructive, heart-breaking lesson. Miraculously, the children did not abandon me, although I felt so dreadful about bringing Don into their lives I wouldn't have blamed them for doing so.

From the beginning Beth told us she did not trust him, but we didn't heed her warnings. While suffering vivid memories of his brutalities, she later wrote the following poem. It is included in tribute to her courage.

> "Pushing his ugly face close to mine
> Whispering his threats
> He tries to make himself feel all powerful.
> But as long as I see through him
> And keep my spirit my own untouched by evil
> I will be free.
>
> I am free and wild
> No threat can ever break my spirit!"

15

CASTING OFF

In the spring of 1972, Beth and I took a short vacation on the Mendocino coast and discovered an inn high above the shore with a path leading down to a small, private cove and beach. There was a huge tunnel rock where the waves came crashing through as well as sunny sand and rocks to explore. We felt we had found a treasure. A couple of months later we returned with Rachel and Kurt.

Since Rachel would be going away to college, we knew this would be our last vacation together for a long time. For me, it was a mixed blessing. Our years of doing things with the children living at home were ending, but I was already looking forward to time alone with Kurt. Afterward, when I saw a snapshot taken of us on that trip, I didn't see the hint it gave of his true feelings. I am smiling happily into the camera—he is looking away, with strain written all over his face. Later, we shared our first bed in years, quietly not touching.

One Sunday when Kurt and I were alone, we began planning a new landscaping project and I felt a sense of companionship rekindling. Details of that day stand out clearly in my memory. I felt we were on the threshold of a new life together—not unlike my feelings when we were first married.

We were designing a rock garden with a little stream coming out of the woods behind our house. After a while we drove down to Redding to see a similar one. Then on the way home we stopped in to visit with friends, who had been making landscaping changes in their surroundings. It was a beautiful day. And I felt light-hearted in the pleasures and plans we were sharing.

After we came home and while going up the front steps, Kurt calmly said, "I have something I want to tell you." Instantly I knew it was all over. I had no idea what he wanted to tell me, but I felt certain that our marriage was ending.

We went inside to the dining alcove at the end of the kitchen. Silently, Kurt watched me pour fresh coffee into our old familiar mugs and place them on the table. We sipped our coffee and I held my breath.

Kurt looked down into his mug, then away, and said, "I feel sorry to tell you this, Barb, but I care for someone else." Without pausing he told me that it was someone he had known for many years.

Spinning—falling—fast

"Even though she lives near Los Angeles, we have been writing and seeing each other for quite awhile."

Hitting bottom—it's really over!

"When? How?" I managed to ask.

"The camping trips I took to Big Sur were not with the guys, as I said they were. We went to other places too, when you thought I was just visiting relatives." He rushed on, "Her husband knows and he's okay about it."

But I'm not okay at all.

"You mean you want us to go on being married?" I asked. "Does she know you're telling me?"

Slowly, he answered, "Yes, she does. And she doesn't want us to change anything."

A tiny spark flickered back, "I can't pretend something that's not true, Kurt. I don't know what we'll do, but we can't go on together now," I said with a conviction that surprised us both.

"Oh gosh," he protested, "she doesn't expect us to separate. Why can't we just continue as we are?"

"Because it feels wrong—that's all I can say." He looked confused.

Presently I wondered about their letters and asked, "Did she address them to the office?"

"No, she sent them to Frank at his home and he gave them to me."

Doubly betrayed! What must Kurt have said to get him to agree to this?

As I thought back to the last time I'd seen Frank, I asked, "How long has she been writing to you through him?"

He read my hurt and responded casually, "Oh, I don't know exactly—a couple of years or more."

Oh my God!—I wish I could disappear.—I'm so ashamed.

The length and deception of this affair began to sink in—extinguishing the tiny spark. Then suddenly Kurt looked bleak and sad about hurting me, and I found myself feeling crazily sorry for him—not angry. But he was resolute in wanting to continue their relationship.

"She means a lot to me and we want to go on seeing each other. I hoped that you and I could go on as we are, but if not, well—I'm sorry because I don't want to give her up. We wanted you to know, though, so we could be open about it, like we are with her husband. We hoped you'd understand."

He still looked bleak.

Why does he look the way I feel?

I felt incapable of coping with this—the ultimate rejection—that of my husband, my friend since childhood, the father of my children. Two monumental waves washed over me. The first one was an enormous sense of guilt for the way I had treated him, which caused him to seek comfort and support elsewhere. When I brought Don into our lives, Kurt had reason enough to turn away from me.

The second wave was feeling an enormous sense of loss—of a person I had cared for in one way or another most of my life; and the loss of a marriage that never had a chance to plumb its depths, overcome mutual hurts, and bloom as I'd dreamed it someday would. Just at the time I thought it was moving in that direction, it was finished. I felt as though I had been walloped from behind, flattened face down, and cast adrift.

I moved to the chaise lounge in the patio. It was facing away from the house—toward the shadowy woods, and I felt myself pulled deep within them. Several hours later when Rachel returned from a visit with her friends, I was still sitting there. She joined me, bringing out two glasses of lemonade. As she sat down I knew by her cheery manner that she wanted to chat. But I couldn't take my eyes off the woods—even long enough to greet her.

Immediately she asked, "Mom, is something wrong? What is it?"

I don't remember what I said—only how I said it. I couldn't look at her.

In a monotone that sounded as though it came from far away, I told her that her dad cared for someone else. I laid no blame anywhere—then—I just told her the facts as Kurt had told me.

She was appalled, dazed, but rallied and quickly expressed her concern for me. Later, she urged me to eat something, and gently took over until I went to bed. I stared at the ceiling all that first night—a numb body with a blank mind—unable to close my eyes or move until morning.

After that I began to function as though in a trance. It never occurred to me to cry. I wasn't even close to crying, until after I began to work at the hospital the next afternoon. Even then, it was totally unexpected. Tears began to fall with the approach of a co-worker I hadn't known very well. When I saw her coming down the hall, I suddenly felt that my whole world was gone. Nothing would ever be the same, I knew, including my work associates. I irrationally assumed that I would have to disappear from Redding and start over somewhere else. I felt too disgraced to remain there. Mercifully, the supervisor gave me a few days off to pull myself together, before I made any rash decisions.

My initial impulse to flee the community evaporated, for I knew I didn't have the courage or the strength to seek a new job, in a new area, right then. One major change at a time was enough. We put our large home on the market and it quickly sold. We bought a smaller one for me, nearer to the hospital where I worked, and Kurt rented a cottage.

Although the house was twelve years old, it was painted light yellow with white trim and had a refreshing, new look. With a fireplace and swimming pool, it was comfortable and enjoyable in all seasons. On an open hill overlooking Redding, there was a lovely view of Mount Lassen beyond. And at sunset the mountains glowed pink, then darkened to purple; moonrises were stunning and the clear air made stars appear within reach.

It was such an unexpected bonus to find this perfect place, I could hardly believe that the calamitous event which precipitated it had actually occurred. But as the family was leaving on moving day, granddaughter Megan suddenly turned back to say, "Oh Granny, when we go you'll be all alone." She looked so distressed that I had to find a grin for her and words of reassurance for us both.

The months following my move were filled with confusion for all of us. I felt that our feelings were beyond sorting out—that all our family relationships (not just Kurt's and mine) had changed—and that I would never again be certain about them. It felt as though we had been living with veiled emotions in a house of cards all those years. Nothing had been solidly based, and now it had all tumbled down.

Because I felt angry, guilty, and fearful about the end of my marriage, I was prone to feel angry about everything else in my life. Although I sounded like the injured party when I talked about Kurt, inwardly I felt guilty. For I really believed that this marriage failure was primarily my fault.

I had been the temperamental one and Kurt had been the stable one who had kept our sinking ship afloat, I told myself. Unconsciously, I shoved aside memories of his painful abuses and his flight from intimacy, as I assumed I deserved his punishments.

As summer approached the following year, I decided to return to the little inn at the coast with its private cove. I knew I'd be haunted by memories of our family's previous visit, but the urgency to experience it alone overrode my apprehensions.

I had a tiny upstairs room, looking across the bluff to the ocean. There was no television, radio, or phone. I felt myself abandon the usual trappings of my life. Sponge-like, I soaked up the simple atmosphere of this appealing coastal village, as I relaxed and slept soundly for the first time in months. Perhaps to the inhabitants it was not as free of problems as it appeared, but to me it was uncomplicated and perfectly met my need for rest and refuge.

Although it had been a long time since I had felt the urge to write, I walked down to the shore one morning, carrying paper and pen. Since it was stationery, perhaps my initial intention was to answer letters, but that was not what happened.

On reaching the sand, I sat watching the waves and then some divers in wet suits, who appeared in a small boat from somewhere beyond the cove. After they were gone, the warm June sun invited me to relax. I stretched out and listened to the waves. I was completely alone, and felt gently mingled with the sea, sun and sand. My mind free-floated—a lovely relief—and I slept for a time.

When I awoke I was suddenly conscious of things falling into place. And I began to write. Answers to questions I wasn't aware of asking seemed to flow through me, organizing themselves as they revealed themselves. None were on a philosophical or spiritual level; they concerned my current problems and goals and gave me practical step-by-step ideas for solutions. They were written in a small, neat hand which tells me that the material came to me systematically, pushing through any judgmental controls which could have impeded them. It was my first encounter with ideas and guidance emerging from my subconscious and it was very exciting.

This experience at the shore was a breakthrough. It occurred as I sought escape from seemingly endless floundering, and showed me that beneath the turmoil existed the clarity and common sense I needed. I could cope.

I saved the papers and reviewed them occasionally in the following months to take my bearings and adjust my course. In the years since, I have returned to the inn and its cove several times, with fond memories of that earlier visit, when I first saw a dimension of my self that I didn't know I had.

At first, it was hard to accept the notion that I had only myself to please in planning my surroundings. Actually, it gave me a starting place for self discovery.

Prolonged disorder wore me out just by being there, but the new thrust I was sensing to improve my home environment didn't come from this old attitude.

It had to do with color, fabric, mood, and discovering what combination of these elements promoted my sense of being in a special place—one that would be nurturing. With little to spend on materials, I enjoyed the challenge of bringing nondescript rooms to life. Colored sheets and nature calendar photographs worked miracles.

To decorate for my psyche was a new experience—a huge step away from the practicality of floors clean enough for crawling babies, and furniture designed to survive as the babies grew bigger. Now, even though the users of linoleum and Naugahyde were gone, my heart still clung to those early years. And our familiar furnishings stood there as silent sentinels to intensify my sad and lonely feelings.

Gradually I began to get rid of everything. At the time it felt instinctive and I didn't look too deeply into what prompted each decision. At first I felt guilty about buying things, but later as they began to go together and I could see the ME being expressed, it became fun. I allowed myself to enjoy using them—all by myself—for the first time in my life. I was fifty-two years old.

After the initial shock of becoming separated had subsided, Kurt and I found that we were able to return slowly to our pre-marital friendship. We discussed common problems, such as car maintenance, care of the house, and we continued to share our checking account. But I never felt secure about my financial future, should our separation become permanent, and Kurt seemed uninterested in helping me figure out a concrete plan.

In spite of nagging unease over this issue, I tried not to let it interfere with other aspects of our life. I wanted him to feel welcome to share visits and holidays with the children, and there was an unusually pleasant period of several months when we tackled replacing the large deck around the house. We did the work together.

Although the enlightenment I received in the cove had given me a glimpse of self help, I was still a long way from self understanding. I continued to be swept by recurring feelings of inadequacy, depression, and alienation.

Inwardly thrashed by a rising sense of insecurity, I wasn't able to conceal the turmoil in my daily life. It shoved its way into my job relationships and caused stresses I couldn't understand or handle effectively. Eventually, as my self confidence crumbled, I decided I wasn't suited for nursing in an acute care facility and began to seek an alternative. Initially I attended innumerable workshops and seminars, feeling I needed more education and training to pursue another nursing focus.

Thirsty for workshops that would help me grow personally and professionally, the idea of individual counseling and therapy to achieve these goals was still foreign to me. I couldn't talk about internal, private matters with anyone. Since I didn't associate those hidden aspects of myself with career difficulties, I kept pursuing the only course I knew anything about—trying to fit square me into a round hole. I was willing to try to become round, but didn't know how.

During these troubling years I found encouragement and comfort in the songs of Anne Murray. She entered my life when I was alone, drifting, not knowing how to reach out for help—or where to look for it. I saw her picture on a Canadian magazine cover and read about her before I ever heard her sing. Something clicked and later with her "Snowbird" I felt I had found an old friend.

Through her magical voice and variety of moods, I began to find my self—the young woman-me—who had so much locked up inside and had lost the keys many years before.

Who can say who our guides in life will be or how they will help us? I only know that for several years she was mine. She helped me bear the unbearable and move on.

After a while I began to realize that I would never feel at home in Redding. I had made some new friends after Kurt and I separated, but resisted becoming close to anyone.

There was one final factor overriding the others, which heightened my sense of vulnerability and isolation. Because the part of town where I lived was being plagued with burglaries, a number of us contracted for alarm systems in our homes directly connected with the Police Department.

Not long after mine was installed, my modest home was "hit" while I was out of town. The police responded promptly and caught the burglars. But because they were juveniles who hadn't had time to take anything, their identities were never disclosed and nothing came of it.

Some months later when I returned from a meeting I found the police were surrounding my house. The silent alarm had gone off, but apparently the intruders recognized the system, because they left without being caught, and took nothing.

After the police had gone, I fell apart. I had come to the end of the line. In the silent house, an ominous threat hung in the air. I undressed for bed, but began walking back and forth, unable to stop.

Soon, the helpless child deep inside, who had been powerless to prevent the assaults of her father, was gripped by terror. As I paced the floor for several hours, I felt certain I was losing my mind.

Finally I called a friend about two a.m. who came over and urged me to seek help—professional help. "You may not believe this, but you are very strong," Geri said. "Now you are using all your strength to keep something down and out of your range of awareness, but if you could let yourself into it and explore the pain, you could use your strength to work through it. Then you'd begin to come together again and feel better."

I was surprised at the depth of her insight. But it was hard to accept her advice because I didn't know what I was repressing. In the years that followed, I've come to fully appreciate the fact that she was right on target.

"You can't explore the ocean unless you have the courage to lose sight of the shore."

Quoted by Diane Sawyer
CBS Morning News
June 4, 1984

Despite Geri's encouragement, I felt there was no professional in that area that I could confide in, so I made arrangements to leave. I sold my home and gave up my job. At the same time, I decided that my four year separation from Kurt had outlived its usefulness. We were not going to resume our lives together, and the end of the marriage needed to be formally acknowledged. I knew this would be financially risky, but I didn't know how else to resolve our situation.

I had agonized endlessly over letting go, caught in the incest survivor's desperate pattern of hanging onto the only reality I knew. Because I had learned when I was little to make the best of the insecure relationships I had with my parents, it was the only response pattern I had to draw on. For me, staying with it "for better or for worse" began in childhood, not when I married.

Although I knew my fear of letting go went much deeper than the financial risk, I didn't understand it then, and hoped I would overcome it eventually. I was also very tired of feeling stuck in an unresolved limbo.

After twenty-five years of marriage and nine years in Redding, I gave up; we were divorced, and I returned to Sonoma County, where I had spent most of my life. Karin and her daughter Megan were there—I longed to be near them. Since I had no job or home, though, I felt I was returning to another abyss. Everything that represented stability in my life was disappearing and I was unable to stop the process. But the move brought me to the help I desperately needed. It was indeed time to "explore the ocean."

AFTER A WHILE

After a while you learn the subtle difference
Between holding a hand and chaining a soul,
And you learn that love doesn't mean leaning
And company doesn't mean security,
And you begin to understand that kisses aren't
      contracts
And presents aren't promises,
And you begin to accept your defeats
With your head held high and your eyes open,
With the grace of a woman, not the grief of a child.
You learn to build your roads
On today because tomorrow's ground
Is too uncertain for plans, and futures have
A way of falling down in mid-flight.
After a while you learn that even sunshine
Burns if you get too much,
So you plant your own garden and decorate
Your own soul, instead of waiting
For someone to bring you flowers.
And you learn that you really can endure,
That you really are strong
And you really do have worth
And you learn and learn . . . and you learn
With every goodbye you learn.

Veronica A. Shoffstall © 1971

PART THREE

"The first flash of consciousness reveals so much that it seems like the sun coming up. In fact, it's more like a first candle in the dark."

Gloria Steinem
***OUTRAGEOUS ACTS AND
EVERYDAY REBELLIONS***

16

THERAPY BEGINS

Spring 1976

After the divorce, confusion and fear were the only feelings I could clearly identify. Although I missed my children, I refused to consider loneliness—even to myself. I didn't know that I was depressed. Since guilt pervaded my emotional life, there was no room for me to feel anything else.

My supportive and wise physician advised me to undertake therapy thinking my divorce had triggered the depression. He asked the Mental Health Department to see me promptly, which helped me get started. At last I could begin to discover what was the matter with me, and learn how to survive.

I soon found myself in a sunny, cheerful room with Margaret—a quiet, attractive woman—younger than me, but old enough to inspire my confidence. During our first appointment she concentrated on learning about my family and my life in general. I didn't know how all that connected with my present unstable situation and was extremely wary of looking into my childhood for answers. No matter how uneasy I had felt with my parents, I couldn't allow myself to think that there was anything abnormal about them. The possibility of their having had an adverse effect on my life seemed unlikely to me. Fortunately, Margaret knew more about emotional healing than I did.

In giving my history to her I briefly touched on my relationship with my father and confessed (appropriate verb, because that's the way I felt about it—guilty) to the incest. When she tried to help me look at it more closely, I resisted. I wasn't ready to lance that boil, but she quietly set the stage.

During therapy sessions, while I was struggling with the present, I would unemotionally answer occasional questions about my childhood, but I never felt they were important enough to pursue, and Margaret never pushed them. Later, in between sessions, forgotten or previously undervalued segments of my life and relationships would float up to the surface of consciousness. I was now forced to confront my memories which I found incredibly hard to do. But, ultimately, this was as useful as it was painful, for it put me on the road back through my life that I needed to take.

When I finally began to discuss my early years with Margaret, I felt no anger. I just calmly acknowledged the hurts and abuses and related their occurrence. But during this same period I would get furious over current slights; inconveniences caused by a store, for instance, whose sale items were all gone on the first day, or other superficial irritations. Mild annoyance would have been appropriate, but I was furious.

Margaret helped me cope with these and more serious levels of chaos in my life right then and it was good to be with someone who could hear my despair but inspire me to overcome it.

The early months of therapy were like being on a roller-coaster, though, between a painful present and a veiled past. My progress continued to be out of focus to me and difficult to identify. I often felt that it was too late for therapy, and I was becoming too tired to keep on trying. I was fifty-six years old and missed the long-ago married feelings of being a wife and part of a lively, growing family. Some days life seemed barely tolerable.

The more I tried to accept the divorce, the less clear were its causes. It was like trying to find a ring in the soft mud under water at the edge of a lake. The more I groped, the muddier the water became and I knew the ring was sinking deeper with each attempt to locate and retrieve it.

One day I found myself wondering if the failure of my second marriage was in any way related to the first marriage failure, although my two husbands were so dissimilar. My first marriage was not an altogether unhappy experience, but I never felt that I knew Jerry very well. For many years I marvelled at my lack of a sense of our having ever been married. It was more like a dream than real life. When it ended, it faded—almost as though it had never been.

But my feelings about my second marriage and my pain after it ended were just the opposite. Reminders of our long relationship, especially the good times, occurred daily for years and continued to follow me everywhere. Unable to fully accept our divorce, I continued to resist the resolution of my feelings about it for years.

So my depression hung on, while I fought all the symptoms— lethargy, insomnia, edginess, inability to concentrate—and hoped the world didn't notice how weird I felt most of the time. I had no understanding of the turmoil hiding beneath my depression.

Some years previously I had made two unsuccessful attempts to learn the opinions of physicians about incest and briefly shared (without details) that it had happened to me. The first was with the physician to whom I was engaged, and had disastrous results, as I have already described. The second tentative step was taken almost twenty years later, during my second marriage. I was feeling Kurt's rejection and wondered if, because of the incest, something was permanently wrong with me. The doctor was embarrassed, gave me no information or reassurance, and I determined never to bring up the subject again.

I'm certain that Margaret noted my flat, brief, unemotional statements when incest was first mentioned between us. It was certainly not related to my present predicament, I naively believed.

When we did begin to discuss Dad's abuses I was surprised to hear that it could be important to look into them more fully. When I described a particularly humiliating occurrence, Margaret would say things like, "That would make me very angry." I felt only wonder and surprise. Anger was an appropriate response? Then why hadn't I felt it? Why didn't I? As I drove home afterward, my inner voice would cry,

Oh, to be clear and angry, instead of confused and lost!

I also felt at fault for not being angry when it happened, and not stopping my dad then. Margaret, in trying to put me in touch with my buried rage, didn't intend to exacerbate my sense of guilt, but I believe that it couldn't be helped. I had lived with a highly developed guilt complex since childhood and wasn't going to let go of it easily. It always gripped me whenever any other feelings tried to emerge.

One day at home I experienced a tearing in the curtain between me and my hidden anger. I had bought a Helen Reddy recording because her song, "I Am Woman" helped me feel stronger and better about myself. But when I first heard her sing, "Leave me alone—why don't you leave me alone?" I was instantly transported back to the child-me, and in my heart I was screaming those words at my smirking, seductive father. I sang them with the record—over and over—and felt they had been written for me—to give voice to the anguish and anger I was just discovering was there.

Although when it happened I knew nothing about flashbacks, that's what it was—"the first flash of consciousness" of child-me feelings. I knew I had seen "the first candle in the dark."

One afternoon with no provocation, I suddenly became a monster. I started yelling and throwing things all around Margaret's office. I felt wild—uncontrolled—strong and furious. I wanted to destroy everything in sight and didn't care what I broke. Even living plants became targets and missiles as I hurled them around the room.

I was enraged and felt awful, but I was also scared and out of control. I couldn't stop myself—hated what I was doing—and, for a time, didn't want to stop myself. These mixed violent feelings appalled and terrified me.

Margaret stood by, allowing my furies to run their destructive course, and afterward I felt abysmally ashamed. We may have discussed it later, but I don't remember having any understanding of why it had occurred. Like a raging firestorm, it left only devastation in its wake.

I couldn't shake the puzzling memory of Margaret's standing aside—waiting for the storm to pass—instead of getting in there and working with me to find its source so that I could put it out, or channel it somehow. It was like the time when I was six and couldn't swim, and Mother continued to chat with a friend beside the pool where I was drowning. I couldn't get her attention and a stranger rescued me. This time I wanted to rescue myself, but I couldn't see my enemy.

I think I was too much for Margaret at times. Although she was not afraid of my anger, she didn't seem to know what to do with it, or how to help me deal with it once it showed itself. For me, being out of control was terrifying and I no longer felt safe with Margaret. I felt crazy.

Thinking about this incident several years later, I wished that she had gotten me to express what I was feeling right then. Never mind why, or at whom, but WHAT—rage—fear—hate—WHAT WAS I FEELING?! (Much later I realized it was a missed opportunity—a chance to meet my anger head on, validate it, own and respect it as a necessary part of becoming a whole person.) Margaret must have known that my anger stemmed from my feelings about my father and the incest and could have provided me with this feedback. Even if I hadn't believed this explanation then, it could have cleared the way for me to believe it later on. (I also wished that she had given me pillows on which I could safely punch out my rage. This is what I finally did recently at a workshop for incest survivors, so I know it works.)

Early one morning four years later, an explanation occurred to me that made the whole thing plausible at last. There in Margaret's office I was suddenly re-experiencing the time my father broke my precious little Japanese puzzle box. As I broke something of Margaret's, I was my father with all his pent-up feelings. At the same time I was myself, avenging his destruction of my prized possession with its secret compartment, and its symbolic twin which he also destroyed—my childhood sense of personal purity, my self respect.

Margaret in her passive non-intervention was playing my role of the speechless child, looking on helplessly while the box was being destroyed. She was also acting like my mother—unwilling or unable to rescue me from my father. I despised their dual female helplessness (like my own) for feeding my rage. With this clarity came a sense of relief, and I could finally let go of that frightening scene.

It had been two years since I had left Redding and begun therapy. I was enjoying nursing, and the opportunity to work closely with patients and their families. It was wonderful to be able to set my own problems aside, to feel totally present when I was with them, and to have my skills needed, available and appreciated. I also enjoyed the friendliness and cooperation of my co-workers, but after a while I began to feel overwhelmed by the demands on me, and some of us were discouraged by the short-staffing we were expected to overcome. In addition, I was feeling buffeted by the emerging emotions I was experiencing in therapy.

I struggled on for a couple of months until I woke up one morning with a painfully stiff neck. Somehow I got to my doctor. After a few days it eased enough for me to move about and drive, although my neck still felt frozen. But despite the strain I wanted to keep working and my co-workers welcomed me back. Their warmth was encouraging and I told myself that I felt better each day.

One afternoon soon after I returned to work, I was called into the Nursing Director's office. Without warning, she smiled and said, "I'm taking you off the regular schedule and placing you 'on call.' I think that's best, don't you?"

Crashing inside, I told her, "I can't make it financially if I go on call. There must be another way for me to stay on as a regular part-time employee." She said that would not be possible.

Hoping for time to find something else I asked, "When will the change become effective?"

"Next week." I couldn't believe it, but that was the end of that.

17

FIGHTING BACK

Spring 1978

With the abrupt finale of my career as a nurse and no idea of what I would do next to survive, I decided that no matter how distasteful the thought was, it was time to begin fighting back. So I filed a complaint for workers' compensation against the hospital.

The case dragged through a variety of appointments, correspondence and two physical examinations. All of them increased my sense of unending struggle, partly because my lawyer's support seemed only tentative. I never did feel at ease with him.

One day I had an appointment with a physician in San Francisco, to whom I was sent by my lawyer, and on whom I depended for a favorable report. I expected him to be professional, empathic and skillful. Instead I found a very large, overbearing man who made sarcastic remarks about other patients to his secretary. As I sat before his desk, I began to have misgivings.

During our interview, I was puzzled by his efforts to impress me with his professional qualifications. Afterward his secretary told me to undress and put on the little open-backed gown provided. Since I thought that it was to be only a neck examination, I was surprised by this request, but when told that the examination would be thorough enough to rule out any other contributing factors, I complied.

After she disappeared, the doctor came in. He must have read uncertainty in my expression, because he brusquely commented about her presence being unnecessary. I felt foolish for being embarrassed, and too unsure of myself and afraid of him, to have anger even occur to me.

Although he didn't touch me inappropriately during most of the examination, I felt like a small child—under a bully's threat. But I couldn't trust my own perceptions. Was I being ridiculously self-conscious? Was parading around the room with my backside exposed necessary? Was I over-reacting to his strange, haughty manner? I had no answers.

He concluded his inspection by standing me in the middle of the room for a special "heart test." By this time I was beyond questioning anything he did, so I stood as instructed. He had me put my hands down at my sides—I couldn't hold my gown together. Then he placed himself behind me, wrapped me tightly in his huge arms, pressed his body firmly against my naked back, and listened to my chest with his stethoscope.

> *This can't be happening—Oh God, he's thick and strong!*

Next he had me face him,

> *Please no! Not this way—*

and pulled me firmly against him,

> *Spinning—sinking—caught in a nightmare—can't move—*

The stethoscope on my back—his chest pushed against my cheek—

> *Taking so long—Please have it over—*

Going home on the bus, feeling utterly destroyed, I debated reporting him to my lawyer, but decided against it. I felt dependent on both of them and feared they would stand together, discounting anything I said as the ravings of a distraught woman.

I learned later that victims of prior abuses (especially of childhood incest) are easily trapped by the power of subsequent abusers. But I didn't know this at the time of that fateful appointment. Sometime after the case was settled I learned that the doctor had killed his wife and then committed suicide. How many other vulnerable victims had he amused himself with, I wondered, while collecting enormous fees for his unprofessional "services"?

When the case was all over, I felt that the small settlement didn't begin to repay me for the indignities in his office that day—to say nothing of my original complaint against the hospital. I felt betrayed by the whole long process—tired and powerless. I wanted only to forget it.

Rehabilitation counselling helped me to choose a new career, one that interested me and was different from anything that I had tried before. I began training to be a travel agent. But during those next strenuous months, my attention was divided between my training and Susan's daughter, Amy.

Susan and her family had recently returned to Sonoma County. She had divorced and remarried, but continued working to help support her three children. Amy, the middle child between her brothers, was lithe and small-boned—growing gracefully into her teens.

The previous year I had spent a few days with them and I was still troubled by memories of that visit. I had a vague apprehension that Amy's stepfather was teasing her in a cruel, unhealthy way. He would taunt her until she cried and then make a big fuss over her, coaxing her to make up with him. Sometimes he ridiculed her for crying. Amy had always been a cheerful, cooperative, responsible youngster, more than willing to help at home, and eager to learn in school. During my visit, it was painful to see her made unhappy by this insensitive man, but beyond that a bigger alarm was ringing inside me, although I couldn't identify it specifically. A year later it was ringing again, even though Amy no longer cried.

One day when I was preoccupied with concern for her, I turned on the television to watch Cecil Williams' program "Vibrations." I had known him since we worked on a Methodist Church committee about fifteen years before, and had come to value his insights. That day the topic was incest and his guest, Sandra Butler, had just written a book on the subject, *Conspiracy of Silence*. It was the first time I had heard my private demon discussed in public and I hung on every word.

What a revelation it was to learn that the abuses of my childhood continued to affect every aspect of my entire life! It was hard to believe that I was not to blame for the incest, since I had felt guilty for as long as I could remember. But as I began to recognize the manifestations of the damage, I couldn't avoid acknowledging the connection, no matter how difficult it was to shed the pervasive, clinging sense of guilt.

While these truths were slowly taking root, I began developing strong convictions about the destructiveness of incest. This led to my sickening awakening to the idea that some of my own children may also have been harmed, not by my dad—I didn't suspect him—but by others; for example, my brother Lee who had molested Karla some years before. Although I knew I couldn't undo their pain, I wondered if I could belatedly help them. I was finally breaking through the enveloping numbness that had inhabited and inhibited my senses for so long and prevented me from discussing sexual matters with my children while they were growing up.

Soon I began to sense harmful sexual undercurrents in the relationships between other adults and children, even though I had no concrete evidence or information. I began to realize that the acute unease I felt in Amy's home was a replay of past fears—long buried—sexually oriented, and still beyond my comprehension. I became so unnerved by these unconfirmed anxieties that I thought of little else and slept hardly at all. One night in the twilight zone between awareness and sleep...

> *A door is opening on a darkened room. With temporary night blindness. I am peering inside. I'm appalled by what I see as my eyes become accustomed to the dim light. The child is struggling alone—and losing. She gives up. He has her.*

With this frightening mind-scene I suddenly felt the reality of an abuser's raw control, and had a clearer focus on Amy's plight. In a sinister way she was being broken down, despite her strong efforts to resist him. Most recently her stepfather wanted to take her places she didn't want to go—to concerts or meetings where he could be alone with her before they returned.

Susan appeared oblivious of the disaster that was overtaking her child. In fact, she encouraged Amy to be nice to her stepfather and "not hurt his feelings."

I felt all alone with my mounting anxiety. I didn't know that my own confused childhood had seriously affected my parenting instincts with my children. But Susan was now exhibiting the same denials of reality that she had received through me as a child; she lacked the awareness that could have alerted her. And I still couldn't be direct with her.

But I couldn't ignore my alarm. During therapy, I told Margaret about my fears for Amy and I spoke with a local crisis clinic. Their responses were identical: since I hadn't seen anything sexual occurring, nothing could be done.* I knew it was highly improbable that I would ever see anything, but I felt that something horrendous was about to happen, and my helplessness to stop it was consuming me. I was certain that if I tried to warn Susan about her husband I would be unwelcome in their home, so I could only encourage Amy to call me if she needed me. I didn't dare be more candid.

Feeling frightened and ineffectual, I sent for Sandra Butler's book. It brought my first knowledge of my "sisters" out there, and the reassurance that I was no longer alone in my lifelong confusion. It

---

*This was before the California law mandating reports of suspected abuse.

provided concrete information about the depth and extent of incest, and validated my apprehensions about Amy's plight.

Then suddenly her family was torn apart. Someone I didn't know called and told me to park outside Susan's apartment building and wait. In a few moments Susan and the children came rushing out, jumped into the car, and in a strong, low voice Susan said, "Drive, Mom—just drive away—anywhere!" I lived seven miles away, so we went home to my apartment.

There, far more than my worst fears about Amy's stepfather were confirmed. While Susan was at work he had not only been molesting her himself—he had been "preparing" her for others. Susan learned of his plans just in time to prevent his taking Amy to "the streets" of Hawaii. That evening they escaped while he was out.

But in the upheaval of fury, heartache and confusion after we came to my home, Amy ran away. While we searched for her ourselves, we also enlisted the police who were quick to respond. After a couple of anxious hours, a police officer found her, and I went down to pick her up.

We all spent the rest of the night in the police station, where the dreadful story had to be told. The officer in charge was unusually sensitive in the way he questioned Amy and handled her case.

In the morning we went with the police to Susan's apartment to collect their things. The stepfather was there, but he collapsed, crying, on the couch when he saw the police. My stomach was churning as I watched him curl up in a fetal position—making high moans that didn't sound human. When the police took him into custody, there was no roughness—no harsh exchanges. None were needed. They were in charge and professional; I felt sick inside, but safe.

Later I became so unstrung with rage about Amy's desecration, and my own impotence in preventing it, that I wrote to Sandra Butler. She graciously responded, offering support and the opportunity to meet. But I wasn't ready to touch my uncontrollable anger again. I tried to rise above it, when I really needed to scream in a safe place.

However, I couldn't escape. During a (confidential) group therapy session, I began talking about Amy's plight. When someone said, "She could have stopped him," my lid blew completely off. I was infuriated by the implication—disbelief in Amy's innocence. By innuendo, the remark also invalidated all the efforts I had made to shed my own guilt. I was only just beginning to believe in my blamelessness, because I believed in Amy's without a doubt. To hold her in any way responsible was intolerable.

I don't know what I expected of the group at that moment, or of Margaret, but I felt so estranged from all of them that I fled. I went directly to the police station and sought the officer who was handling Amy's case. I had lost confidence in everyone else. I felt that only the police shared my rage.

After my initial reactions to the situation had subsided, I felt an urgency to assure that Amy would never again be a victim—of her stepfather, or of the cruel misjudgment of others. I felt that I had to expose the sexual abuse of children as the destructive force it is, and I began by calling a meeting of my daughters. It was time to fight back on a deeper level than ever before.

To assure uninterrupted privacy we met at Eric's home while he was at work. My daughters, all adults by now—some living in other areas—readily made arrangements to come. As we gathered they seemed puzzled but unquestioning, while my unsuspecting sister-in-law graciously welcomed us into her comfortable living room.

The subdued light filtering between the partially drawn curtains lent an air of calmness as I tried to collect my thoughts. It would be the first time I had told in the family about Dad molesting me and I couldn't imagine how it would affect them. I had no way of knowing then that in the years to follow all family relationships would undergo changes beginning on that day.

Since the younger ones hadn't known my dad very well, I wasn't too concerned about their reaction, but I was anxious about Karin, who always seemed to love him. When she did not react at all, I assumed that she was in shock and hoped the truth about her grandfather wasn't too much for her to hear. I didn't recognize that her lack of response was exactly like the numbness which my father's sexual advances had always triggered in me. She was giving me a clue that I couldn't read.

Through the day we discussed as much about sexual abuse and incest as we could. *Conspiracy of Silence* became our first reference for the information we knew we needed and I hoped they would have a better understanding of what had happened to Amy. Sometime later Rachel wrote, "For me what was accomplished by our gathering that day was that I immediately gained a clearer understanding of you, based on what your dad did to you and your disclosure of it all to us. And from there, I started understanding myself a bit more."

Her unexpected acknowledgement was an encouraging bonus. It has served to keep me focused ever since.

"The world is changing so quickly and our values are altering so rapidly that perhaps the only lessons we have for our children are the truths about our own lives—whatever those truths are—for that is all we know."

Sandra Butler
CONSPIRACY OF SILENCE

18

COLLISION WITH REALITY

January 1980

Late one night I was lying in bed, sleepless. In hopes of finding some inconsequential diversion, I turned on the bedside television and prepared to fall asleep to a talk-show program. By unknown design, I tuned in to an interview with a therapist who had written a book about incest and was accompanied by some of her clients.

As the program moved along, I realized that my initial acknowledgement of the abuse that I endured—even the anger and despair I experienced when I couldn't prevent Amy from being assaulted—had only scratched the surface of incest's ongoing effects. I had not really dealt with it in the fighting, all-out manner that I needed to free myself from its grip.

While I watched, riveted by every word, I was shaken by what I was learning about myself. Wide awake and in turmoil, I could not shut my eyes for the rest of the night. Within a few days, I realized that this experience was too much to handle alone. I was on a collision course—with the childhood trauma consuming my ability to deal with escalating present day difficulties.

This time when I sought help I was much clearer about my basic needs, was able to separate the two major struggles in my life, and use the therapy offered more fully than before. After two years of preliminary work, I was at last ready to plunge into the pain.

When I requested and received a counsellor who specialized in incest problems, I hoped that she would help me address my job concerns as well. Sarah was tall and fair—younger than Margaret, but warm and direct. She immediately inspired my confidence.

With her repetition, I finally *felt* clear that I was not responsible for the incest. I was not responsible for the neck problem at the hospital either. I had become a victim of both. Sarah helped me understand how the two problems were linked, and helped me break through my abuse-inviting response patterns.

That winter and spring I rode three wild horses at once: coping with the job I had, trying to secure a new one through endless tests and interviews, and trying to become more in touch with my buried feelings from childhood. I needed a supportive, skillful therapist, and in Sarah I had one.

One afternoon I became so upset at work that something clicked inside. As I was leaving, I felt far away from everyone. Their voices, and even my own, seemed to come from a great distance. Nothing felt real. While I walked to the parking lot, I was shaking, but it felt good to get in the car and close the door. I locked it, then fastened my seatbelt and felt safe in my own private world.

Almost trancelike, I drove slowly through the town. I was fifteen miles from home. On reaching the hills beyond the town, I felt the car go faster. It felt like someone else was inside me and controlling the car. She unlocked my seatbelt. Suddenly I was leaning forward, screaming incoherently, gripping the steering wheel and staring at the winding country road. To my rising horror, I could barely resist the sense of being pulled magnetically to the right—

> *End it now!*
> *No—Not yet—*

and smashing the car into every utility pole,

> *Now—Hurry—Then it'll be over—*
> *No—Not this one—*

along the way,

> *NOW! THIS TIME! THIS POLE!*
> *No—Not yet—*
> *NOW—Not yet—NOW—Not yet—NOW—Not yet—*
> *NOW—Not yet—*

for the entire fifteen miles.

In panic, I went immediately to see Sarah. After talking out the job crisis of that day that had brought on my despair, she suggested that I go to the women's exercise gym I had joined. I worked out on the bicycle and did sit-ups until the rage and tension had dissipated. Then I went home and was soon asleep.

I am absolutely positive that I wouldn't have found the answers I sought or the growth that I needed if I had not resumed therapy with a skilled empathizer that I trusted completely, plus the books that I devoured, one after the other. By jogging my memory and assailing me with my own previously unrecognized feelings as described by some of the authors, I was helped immeasurably. You can trust the hand extended to you when you know that that person has been where you have been. That is what books dealing with incest have meant to me. They were a light shining down into the pits where I was, and then a hand extended to help me climb out.

I began to feel I was part of something that is challenging and affecting change—like a wave starting deep and quiet out in the ocean, growing larger as it rolls over and rumbles powerfully toward shore. To read my own story in the books written by others made me feel part of their cleansing and compelling wave.

Soon I began to understand why I felt as I did about both my parents. I also began to recognize the enormous burden of guilt that I carried—how it wouldn't let me think ill of my father because I needed to look up to him. Instead Mother had become the object of all my anger.

After months of immersion in books about incest, I decided one day it was temporarily time to stop reading them. The words of others had unleashed a torrent of memories and I wanted time to catch up with my own words. They were tumbling out all around me every day and night. I started to record these messages from my unconscious, because I discovered that by doing so my own insights became clearer and more sharply defined. As I moved into this initial phase of healing, I felt Sarah's strong support and encouragement. I was no longer alone.

19

SOURCES OF SUPPORT

On Sarah's invitation I decided to join a group that was exclusively for incest survivors. I felt strange and uneasy when I first met them. They were younger, had been meeting for a number of months, and seemed fond of each other. Because our reason for being together was working through the most personal, private areas of our lives, I wondered about each of them—their childhoods, their abuses, and their parents—but I didn't want to talk about my own. After a while I discovered that differences in incestuous abuses didn't matter. We all had similar scars.

The group was very helpful, in spite of some evident disparities; the main one being my age. We were all there for the same reason, but I was old enough to be everyone's mother—including the leaders'! My better-late-than-never philosophy made me stay, participate, and work—hard. Strong feelings had to surface, be dealt with and released. I had to remember that these women were not my children; we were all fellow sufferers on our way to healing ourselves, and I was soon thankful that they were so much younger—they would not be burdened most of their lives with this unresolved torture. And not only were they working through it as young adults with their lives still ahead of them, most of them had the opportunity to confront their fathers, a step in healing that I did not have.

During this period I learned that we each had found ways to survive incest and its aftermath, even if we hadn't worked through it. Through the others I began to recognize more fully my long and deeply buried feelings of: 1) shame about behavior that I knew was wrong, but was powerless to stop; 2) confusion concerning both my parents; and 3) being soiled and unworthy of my peers. But even when I understood the negative impact of these feelings, I couldn't "think" them out of existence. They were too deep to be altered so easily.

I experienced change as a gradual, uneven, process of release. It involved a great deal of struggling in the dark—trying to find and trust solid ground, sometimes slipping backwards—and at the beginning there was no sense of apparent progress or reward. I felt depressed and awful most of the time for the next couple of years. The only reason I kept going back to therapy was that stopping would have been the end for me, and I knew it.

Sometimes a gloomy mood would creep up on me like quiet fog and envelop me before I knew it was approaching. The temptation to give in, turn on the television and aimlessly mind-drift could become overpowering. One day as this was happening my little inside voice commanded, "MOVE!" and I did. I pushed myself outside to run as far and as fast as I could.

I was delighted to discover such a simple way to chase away the blues and pick up my spirits. My poodle's need for walks provided mood-shakers time and again. Michelle loved to run, and her enthusiastic response to brisk exercise provided the push I needed to get me up, out, and away from inertia and gloom. Exercise became an invaluable tool for me and I developed the habit of engaging in it daily—whether I was depressed or not.

Two special women come to mind when I think of the word "supportive." One was a friend since college, whom I had seen occasionally through the intervening years. We met for lunch one day in San Francisco. It had been a long time since we had gotten together, and it was as happy a reunion as we had anticipated.

I don't know why I was prompted to tell her about the incest. I didn't think of it then as a friendship-tester, but perhaps it really was. To my relief, she came through for me that day with gentle understanding. She was serious, sensitive, and asked none of the questions that would have signalled to me that she doubted my horror story, or my perceptions about its effects.

I found this first experience in discussing incest with another woman outside the family (or therapy) a totally supportive one.

The second special friend doesn't know anything about my childhood. We have never discussed it. One day we enjoyed a picnic together, as we exchanged thoughts about our hopes for changing directions in our work. It was lovely to have her share her own search and doubts so openly.

Afterwards, I received a postcard which began, "Just to let you know how good it was to see you again," and ended, "You are a beautiful person. Please **never** forget. So glad to know you." This spontaneous expression of appreciation and support brought tears to my eyes. Here was someone who had a genuine regard for me—simply as a person.

I received a surprising amount of strength from that powerful little postcard.

During the summer of 1980 I attended a weekend Journal Workshop given by the University of California Extension at the Santa Cruz campus. Frances Heussenstamm, the leader, was a dynamic therapist who in two days opened my eyes to a number of hidden aspects of myself. She was bursting with a contagious vitality as she guided and challenged a large group of men and women to look within, record what they found, and share what they wrote if they wanted feedback.

The process consisted of engaging in written dialogues with a variety of persons (living or dead) and with other aspects of our lives which we personified for the purposes of the dialogues. After she introduced us to a particular topic, we would find separated spaces—indoors or out—and write whatever surfaced as it drew us along. As we did so, the hidden became visible.

These dialogues stimulated significant progress in my self awareness and I am including one with my dad that illustrates my responses to the journal process. It also defines my emotional status at that time, when I felt that my anger toward him was being resolved.

Dialogue With Dad
or
A "Confrontation" 25 years after his death

Introduction spoken to myself (but directed at him) as I watch him approach: I've worked through a lot of painful garbage about our relationship and I wish we had had the chance to confront together the bind you got us into. I feel more mellow toward you now and am able to more fully appreciate what you gave us.

B. Hi Dad! Gee, I've missed you.

D. I've missed you too—you were always special to me.

B. I know I was special and sometimes I liked this, but often I didn't. It was a mixed blessing.

D. I sensed that and didn't know why.

B. I'm not certain why. Perhaps I just hated being different in every way from the boys—not having a sister made me feel alone anyway, and sensing that I was loved differently made me feel even lonelier. And it was strange about you and Mom. It was almost as if the more you cared about me, the less she could. I knew that she wanted to believe she loved me, but I never felt that she did—at least not when I was growing up. Later, after you died, all our relationships changed, but that doesn't really concern you and me now.

D. What does concern us now?

B. I'd like it best if you could tell me.

D. Could you be referring to what happened all those many years ago when I was trying to help you grow up to be a warm, responsive wife?

B. That was the reason you gave me and you told me a lot about Mom when I was little that I've never forgotten, but which I could do nothing about.

D. Was it wrong to share that? I was so troubled. I loved your mother so much and wanted our intimate life to be satisfying for both of us. But she never could allow herself to enjoy it, unless she had psyched herself up to some quasi-spiritual/ aesthetic level—which, after you children were all born, she seldom was able to achieve.

B. But when you told me about it I was just a little girl— hardly mature enough to be able to deal with all that. Maybe it helped you to say it, but I know now it harmed me to hear it.

D. Oh, I don't know, I think you're making too much of it. Why hang onto it? Why don't you let go of it?

B. Why don't you face up to what you *did* as well as what you said? For me, it's all been intertwined all these years. You had many painful years, too—physically and emotionally—but I don't feel responsible for causing you great pain.

D. Are you trying to say that I caused you great pain?

B. I wish to hell you'd own up to it and I wish you had said you were sorry, admitted that you were way off base as a father; admitted that no matter how justified you rationalized your-self into feeling—what you really did was get your kicks at my expense—and it's taken me more than fifty years to come to terms with what you did. Meantime, I was denied the birthright of parents that I could trust. I couldn't trust either of your feelings toward me, and grew up not knowing how to trust anyone—especially myself.

D. God—how awful—I never knew.

B. I wish I'd known much sooner; soon enough for us to talk about it. The mixed feelings for you were so heavy to carry.

Writing this out gave me a wonderful sense of relief.

Almost as suddenly as I had realized months before that I needed to return to therapy, I became aware that my need for the survivors' group was over. Although I knew I had to continue my therapy sessions with Sarah, my decision to leave the group came to me cleanly, without doubt or question. But even though our time of intensive sharing and mutual helping was over, I will never forget those sensitive, gutsy, funny, tender, courageous young women whose pain made them fighters and whose spirit makes them survivors. I owe them a very great deal.

Dear Barb—

I am sending the enclosed note to Karin through you. Please read it and make sure she gets it.

Thanks.

Kurt

20

ONCE IS INEXCUSABLE

August 18, 1980

Dear Karin —

Jeff tells me Megan has reported I raped her at age of ten. It isn't true, but I'm not proud of what did happen:

In the cabin, when we retired to separate beds in separate rooms, she apparently felt uneasy and wanted to crawl in with me. I let her, and when she saw I slept with nothing on, took off her nightgown. She wanted to lay on top of me, and it led to my caressing her and then to her fondling me. That's as far as it went. No force, no aggression, no intercourse. I wouldn't let that happen; I'm not that kind of guy. The only reason it went as far as it did is because I was completely relaxed with wine I had for dinner. I have felt guilty ever since about the effect of my permissive action on the innocent; I also wondered how innocent she really was.

I'm sorry—

Dad

CRASH! How could he?!

I took the letter to Karin. Megan had prepared her, so she wasn't shocked—just sick, and angry.

After Amy's case came to the family's attention, incidents involving others began emerging in bits and pieces. Megan's was among these. By then, she was sixteen and ready to confide her six-year-old secret about her step-grandfather to her shocked Uncle Jeff.

Heartsick, he immediately confronted his father, and Kurt's letter to Karin followed. It revealed, in addition to his account of the incident, a commonly-held misconception about sexual abuse. For in the mind of a child, rape does not have to include penetration by the abuser's penis. She knows she has been assaulted. In fact, the psychological trauma of any type of abuse may be more difficult to heal than the physical damage.

For years, I had considered my brother Lee's abuse of Karla as something apart, in no way connected with Dad's "lessons" about marriage to me. Even Amy's abuse by her stepfather seemed to bear no direct connection to the men in our family. But with this revelation of Kurt's molestation of Megan, I began to wonder why so many of us had become victims of trusted adult relatives in our homes. The tightly-woven fabric of our legacy had begun to unravel.

Somehow, responding to Kurt helped me weather this latest awfulness.

Dear Kurt -

Even though you wrote that intercourse did not occur, all forms of molestation come under the category of incest and are so viewed by the law. **Incest is a crime.** The reason I am informing you about the seriousness of this was triggered by the last sentence in your letter. You wondered just how innocent Megan really was. The facts which define the situation are these:

You were an adult.

She was a minor child—ten years old.

No matter what precedes inappropriate sexual behavior, the adult in the situation is always solely responsible for whatever occurs. To be sure, children feel guilty afterwards because they know instinctively that what happened was wrong. But children lack the wisdom, maturity and power to control or change the situation. **The adult is solely responsible.**

You may feel that since it was only one occurrence, several years ago, it's not worth any further concern on your part. But if you believe one letter will serve to vindicate you, you are mistaken. Megan and Karin have paid and continue to pay a very high price for your lapse in judgment.

Soon after sending Kurt the letter, I called another family meeting. Almost everyone was able to come on the appointed weekend. As we circled ourselves in my living room, some on the floor, it quickly became a painful experience for all of us. There were no smiles and it was hard to talk.

Unlike the first time when I told my daughters about the abuses to Amy and to me, in which the atmosphere was generally calm, sad and thoughtful, this meeting was highly charged—with tears, angry outbursts, and pain, pain, pain.

Kurt conceded that the molest occurred, but tried to minimize its extent by insisting he hadn't raped her. Megan was caught in an agony of semantics, since no word truly described the depth of her trauma. At one point when Karla was crying out her dismay at her father, and another was trying to stop her, I shouted, "Let her cry! Let her cry!" Then I ran upstairs, crying myself, because I wasn't heeded. I still didn't know much about releasing feelings, except that they should be encouraged, not thwarted.

Perhaps in our inexperience with the complexities of a confrontation we didn't handle the situation as helpfully for Megan as we might have, but we did the best we could. She has since told me that the whole experience was devastating. She wasn't certain how others felt toward her, since she was having to describe the dreadful actions of their father.

I was recently touched by her saying that no matter how awful it was or who else doubted her, she always knew that Rachel and I believed her. I'm glad she had that to hang onto, in addition to her mother's loving support. We knew that an assault had been committed and that she had suffered ever since. Her self image was raped.

Despite their concern for Megan, Kurt's children rallied with concern for him as well, although none of us really understood how he could have behaved as he did. But during that entire weekend he was not abandoned for one minute.

As it ended, Karla encouraged him to become better informed about sexual abuse, especially incest, and offered him Sandra Butler's book, *Conspiracy of Silence.* They also discussed the benefits of therapy as a path to emotional health. In his obvious shame, he seemed open and willing to consider their suggestions. I hoped he would follow through, but when everyone was leaving there was an unspoken sadness for a deep sense of loss we couldn't put into words.

Although Megan was too distressed during the meeting to elaborate on the details, Karin told me later that when she returned home that summer six years before, she complained that "Grampa Kurt is a dirty old man." Since she didn't offer any other information, Karin thought she meant that he was being affectionate and that she was embarrassed by his attentions.

Usually a comment like that indicates something is seriously wrong and that the child needs help in bringing out what really is on her mind. But at the time, Karin didn't recognize her child's cry for help. So the nightmare buried itself in Megan's subconscious mind—to take root and undermine her from then on.

During high school she attempted suicide several times—once following a disagreement with a previously admired teacher, who put her out of his class. It was like a repeat of the initial molest and rejection in its impact on her self image, and once again she tried to destroy herself in her despair. Now we were finally beginning to understand the source of this desperate behavior.

In the years following Kurt's and my separation, my employment history had been developing an unfortunate pattern. Time and again I would be off to a good start in a new job that I enjoyed. But then problems would arise that caused me self-doubts, and soon my feelings toward the authority figures on my jobs changed, as I unconsciously associated them with my parents. Their ages (often younger than I) had no bearing. It was their controlling role that generated my sense of vanishing self confidence. If they were impatient or discourteous, I became confused and unable to function adequately. I felt trapped and lost.

Some personnel directors and nursing supervisors with experience and genuine interest, tried to help; others became hostile, authoritarian bosses—from whom I fled to save my sanity. Because I didn't feel strong inside, I gave unconscious invitation to those "bullies" who become scornful in the presence of weakness and react rudely, sometimes cruelly.

Finally, I realized that the underlying cause of my job problems was a basic lack of self-esteem, which caused blocks in my performance. Consequently, I felt unsuited to my work after a while—even a misfit—and didn't know how to overcome the fears of inadequacy that settled over me.

For me, therapy was the key. One day when I tried to thank Sarah for her understanding and help, she wouldn't accept any credit, saying, "You are doing it yourself. Give yourself the credit." That wasn't easy to do when I remembered how badly I was floundering before I knew her. I do know that no one else could make the inner changes for me, but her wisdom and skills were important and her unfailing support was crucial.

The previous eight months' job search had not been successful; but I hung onto the one I had through a number of humiliations until, pushed beyond my limit one day, I left—never to return. Close to collapse and haunted by survival fears, I reluctantly filed a second time for workers' compensation. Eventually, there was a hearing of my case before a judge. The focus, in addition to specifics about my supervisor's unreasonable demands, included emphasis on the fact that I was working through the effects of childhood sexual abuse. The defense asserted that this had impacted adversely on the job relationship.

From the beginning, I had been afraid that the issue of incest might be used against me, but there was nothing I could do about it. When it was over I said to myself, "They can't have it both ways. Since they maintained that my efforts to resolve the childhood problems had affected my job performance and used that to minimize the settlement, *I'll forego minimizing the effects incest has had on my life.* Maybe the exposure of how the system for redressing valid grievances betrays victims will not only help others, it will help me even the score as well. After all, finding oneself a double victim of incest is not something to swallow quietly."

When I talked about this with Sarah, it put me on the road to transcending the pain of the past months and the raw anguish for Karla, Amy and Megan. I began to see this compensation case as a turning point; the final collection of insults it took to free me from my fears about sharing my writing. The focus had cleared. I had to tell our story.

PART FOUR

"Whatever you can do, or dream you can, begin it. Boldness has genius, power, and magic in it."

Goethe

21

THE WAY IN—AND OUT

December 1980

During therapy, I found that writing was a great help—especially in clarifying insights and changes, and in measuring progress. Despite the pain of re-experiencing the past in the midst of a painful present, writing demanded that I go deeper, stay with it, and give up trying to dodge personal problems.

I began with random, unorganized, scribbled notes that I came to refer to as "floaters," because they seemed to emerge from a hidden well deep within me, and float to the surface of my consciousness. As I quickly jotted them down, their pace increased until material was presenting itself almost continuously. When driving, I often pulled off the road to write; I sometimes awakened abruptly and grabbed my pen and pad; I have written on paper towels. It has been a freeing experience to record these floaters.

All along I received them indiscriminately—bits of insights, chunks of memory, and awareness of feelings that surfaced from throughout my life's inner records. Eventually I sorted and filed them according to general topics.

Reviewing them as I put this book together was an absorbing, often difficult process. It required not only rewriting the material, but reliving the content—over and over again. To re-expose myself deliberately to the pain of incest has demanded a total commitment, which I didn't anticipate.

Some months after I'd written about Dad's clitoral molest of me, I re-read that part as an adult looking back on my childhood. With relief I realized that the familiar knot in my stomach and the inner recoiling squirm when those scenes crossed my mind were gone. Writing them down had pulled them out of the child-me, who hadn't been able to let go of them. I'll never forget that they happened, but now when I look back it's like remembering when we moved from one house to another. I don't relive the feelings I had at the time.

On February 27, 1982 I attended a workshop entitled, "Overcoming Fears of Writing and Publishing." It was for women and was led by Ellen Bass, an educator and published writer. I didn't know what to expect, but I knew that I belonged there. In addition to writing and learning from Ellen and from each other, it was a thrill to feel comfortable about sharing something as personal as our writings with women I hadn't previously known.

When Ellen told us that she was editing the writings of victims of sexual abuse in childhood, for a book she hoped would be published, I knew I had been led to her. My first chapters had found their first reader.

Ellen understood that I was overwhelmed at times because in editing her book she, too, had felt overwhelmed by the appalling stories of others. Her anthology, *I Never Told Anyone* was published the following year. It is moving and powerful in its capacity to shatter misperceptions and expose the horrors of sexual abuse.

It helped me understand that the question of harm is not simply one of degree of abuse, but of the fact that abuse occurred at all. Because members of our family were subjected to different types of incestuous abuse, it was important for me to learn that EVERY instance was devastating in its effects. The push I felt to complete my book became inescapable.

2

UNFOLDINGS

I have never been more than an occasional dream recorder. I usually don't even remember them. I did, however, record the following as my unfolding self-understanding led to an increased sense of self worth and some of my old patterns began falling away. Clearly, I was passing through a miracle of changes. This dream was part of the miracle.

I am standing in shadows, near a woman I don't know and Kurt. But they can't see me. He's telling her something about the war-time (WWII) circumstances that led to the marriage of another couple. He's implying that their decision was sudden because they'd known each other only a week, and that they hadn't known what they were doing. (In reality, they have been married more than forty years.)

Presently I realize that Kurt has begun to talk about me—unaware that I am near by. He's saying that my too early first marriage was caused by marijuana—that I didn't know what I was doing either, because I was on dope!

I become furious about his gossipy lie, and quickly step out of the shadows. "My hasty marriage had nothing to do with marijuana," I tell them. "I have never smoked it in my life. Kurt, you have always known, the real reason for my sudden marriage was because I WAS PREG-NANT!" I shout.

The woman turns toward me and looks uncertain. Kurt whirls around and looks embarrassed. Since we had never discussed it, I know I surprised him. I feel suddenly free!

Then I woke up.

Before opening my eyes, I turned this amazing scene over in my mind. How wonderful I felt when I proclaimed the truth in a straightforward manner—without excuses or shame! With a deep sigh, I soaked up all the good feelings. How powerful I felt in the dream and how peaceful I felt afterwards. It was clear to me at last that disclosure can defuse disgrace—no matter how many years it takes.

When I opened my eyes to begin the day, I knew the dream foreshadowed the real life, face-to-face disclosures, with eye contact, that I needed to do. I realized that to feel free of past pain, I had to take responsibility for my own sexual behavior. And I felt a strong push to become as candid when I talked about these issues, as I was when I wrote about them.

This dream broke my family's hold over me by dissolving my shame and vulnerability to innuendoes. I knew I would never feel embarrassed in their presence about those circumstances again.

Part of the process of release from my child-memories of body anguish led me to look into ways to appreciate and enjoy my body as an adult. Although I had always liked vigorous sports, I avoided the plunge into sensual awareness and relaxation gatherings that became so popular during the seventies.

While thumbing through a paper that listed various types of professional services, retreats, and personal growth groups, I realized that I don't like to have things done TO me, such as massages, jacuzzi or even a sauna. I tried to like hot tubs, but couldn't stay in them very long. They made me feel tired and depressed.

It occurred to me recently that I disliked these "relaxer tools" because, in effect, my body was being told to relax. But it was counter-productive. When someone I don't love is touching my body—trying to produce a "letting go" within me, my body cries out, "Leave Me Alone! Why don't you leave me alone?" like Helen Reddy's song.

In the early stages of therapy, when I was beginning to have an awareness of Dad's intrusions on me, I remember telling Margaret that when I first heard that song it brought up the child-me feelings I had when I was alone with him. When I realized that the song fits the feelings I have when I contemplate a massage, I connected the two, understood where these feelings came from and accepted my reservations about massages.

But the automatic numbness I sank into as a child to survive hated touches was a firmly entrenched reaction which prevented my resistance to Dad, or my being able to relax later. So in order to turn around my flight from another's touch, I realized I had to unlearn my blocked responses. This was frightening. I was afraid of restimulating past fears and failures regarding my body. I knew that Dad's betrayal would not be easily overcome, just because I understood it more fully and wanted to outgrow its effects. Although I wasn't ready yet to try, it was becoming clear that the password to enjoyment of another's touch was—trust.

To many the lack of a sexual partner would seem a sterile existence, but I have lived this way for so many years (during marriage and since), that the conscious longing for tenderness and sexual pleasures has waned. I have learned not to reach beyond my own reality.

So, where does that leave me sexually? For some time I had concluded that I would remain completely asexual. I saw this as not only a common situation for many women my age, but for me, a matter of preference. Masturbation didn't lead to orgasm, as it had occasionally years ago; it only brought numbness, anxiety and frustration. I really hated the idea of looking for sexual satisfaction as a single person.

One day I made a surprising discovery. Swimming near the inflow of the pool, I experienced an unexpectedly pleasant arousal caused by the force of the water. Experimenting in the bathtub, I found that the heavy flow of water broke through my sensual numbness. I believe it succeeds because it's a complete departure from the manual path to climaxing associated with urgent fingers. Warm, pleasantly powerful water overcame my old shut-down and brought release. A delightful fantasy soon provided depth to the experience as I felt myself adapt to being human more fully and maturely.

Although I appreciate male friends on a non-sexual level and certainly would not avoid making new ones, I had become intrigued with the new life that was unfolding and didn't miss a sexual relationship. Perhaps one day these attitudes will change. Meanwhile, they feel like soft, warm clothes. They may not be very stylish, but they certainly are comfortable.

23

BABY PICTURES

November 1982

During therapy I came to realize that I automatically used my brain as a barrier to my feelings. I *figured out* the cause of past pains. But I did not *experience* them any more readily in my therapist's office than I had as a child when the shock of betrayal obscured my anger and anguish of loss. I never used the tissues put conveniently within reach by Margaret and Sarah. I didn't hold back tears—they just wouldn't arrive. While I wondered about this, my life in the outside world stumbled on, as Sarah continued to help me cope with it.

Ultimately unable to absorb another rent raise, I moved to a one-room arrangement in the mountains above Napa Valley and rented a storage unit for most of my belongings. One of the cartons held the children's baby pictures. I had not hung them for several years because I was trying to discover other aspects of myself besides my "Mom" role, but they were a constant reminder of the greatest joys in my life. I loved being their mother. By the time I was ready to display the pictures again, I didn't have enough wall space, so put them in storage.

On driving up to my storage unit one day, I noticed a different padlock was on the door. When I couldn't unlock it, I went to the manager's office. He told me there had been some trouble a few days before—that a few of the units had been burglarized and left open without locks, unlike mine which the thieves had replaced to delay discovery.

An ocean's roaring in my head—barely hear him.

After he cut open the unfamiliar lock, I was surprised to see that the unit wasn't completely empty, but also was so stunned that I couldn't remember how it looked when I last saw it. There were empty shelves staring at me—defying me to remember what they had held. A voice in my head began screaming—

I can't stand this! I can't stand this! I can't stand this!

I tried to recall what had been there and soon remembered the carton of BABY PICTURES. It was gone—completely gone! I didn't care about trying to remember anything else, as I dragged myself to the car and began driving up the valley to my home.

Suddenly I knew that I had to see Sarah, I couldn't go on alone. I turned back and hoped to reach her before she left her office. I made it and she saw me immediately.

I don't recall how I told her because from deep inside screams began erupting—like a volcano. But unlike my explosion in Margaret's office, this time I "clicked" and was aware of exactly where it was coming from. I was yelling out my rage at the top of my lungs. Once it began, it seemed to be coming from a bottomless pit and I couldn't stop it. It was like finally being rid of years of nausea in a convulsion of vomiting.

Sarah had won my trust, so when the shock of the burglars' assaults began to hit me, I knew that it was safe to yell unrestrained against all the abusing men in my life. If it blew the roof off the whole building, I didn't care. It felt terrific to scream, "Fuck them all!" at my dad and everyone else who had ever ripped me off. God, it felt good!

Finally, my anger had achieved its rightful place. Finally, it was validated—belonged to me and I was not ashamed of it. Finally, I wasn't afraid to give it voice and let it form itself into the sexual words and obscenities that showed me all the connections I had known in my head, but had not been able to feel in my heart. Finally, my emotional development could begin to catch up with my physical maturity.

It's a sobering experience to be over sixty years old and to meet this deeply feared emotion for the first time as a friend—as a valued partner in my total self. As the rage shoved itself out, power rushed in with more courage than had ever been available to me.

Fury and heartbreak at the senseless losses triggered action. After filing the police report, Karin and I visited the flea markets in two counties and finally found a table with some of my belongings. One still had my name on it in plain sight. With pounding hearts, we quietly bought back the few items displayed, as we tried to appear calm and not arouse the sellers' suspicions. There was a pickup truck behind the table, loaded with cartons and boxes, which I felt certain contained many more of my stolen possessions, including the baby pictures.

We immediately reported to the Sonoma County Sheriff's Department, but because it was a Sunday they were unable to have my police report (in Napa County) verified, so could not search the pickup. They were able to arrest one of the sellers on another charge, but I was not nearly as interested in him as in the contents of his truck.

Karin contacted a friend of hers who came to wait with me until the pickup left the flea market. When we began to follow it, we were spotted, and the woman driver led us on a chase for several hours— over eighty-five miles of county roads. There were two places she ducked into and waited for long periods, and we secured the addresses which I turned over to the detective. In one of these places they located my vacuum cleaner from the registration number. Then the detectives took me there to look for more.

I found a few things, thrown into a filthy house and shed, crawling with mice and crammed in with a huge assortment of property from goodness knows where. In their bedroom closet I found the frames and mats from our baby pictures, but only one photograph of Karin remained, apparently overlooked when they disposed of the others.

The files with my medical, psychological, and employment records were also missing, I soon discovered. With the knowledge that strangers had access to this personal information came the feeling that my insides were parading naked down Main Street. But I really didn't waste any time feeling upset about them. A resignation was setting in about the burglary—an awareness that it was done, and couldn't be undone. My vulnerable privacy, always under siege, couldn't ever be restored, I believed. This led me to feel that no matter how hard I tried to work through my problems I would never be able to overcome my fate as a victim/loser, facing one attack after another.

In looking back I marvel at the healing process I found in writing my way through despair; how I have been turned around and put back on track by insights from within. Alone in my mountain room one night, I wrote:

"Sometimes as the waves of anger and sorrow rush over me, when I remember the pieces of my life that have vanished, I sense a push from an unseen force. It's as though something is trying to erase me from the universe—is trying to deny me my sense of belonging here and is obscuring my rightful place in the scheme of things.

"My mind tells me this is not so, but when I'm tired my strength ebbs and my inner self can't ignore the question. Perhaps I need these crushing waves now and then to stiffen my resolve; to dig in my heels in defiance; to get on with my work and to finish it, despite all setbacks.

"Suddenly I don't care anymore who knows what about me. I will write freely and continue to use my own name. My life belongs to me!"

After the robbery triggered that first breakthrough of identifiable rage, a quiescent period followed, in which I sensed that my feelings for Dad were settling down. I began thinking of him and myself as troubled persons—no longer dominated by incest—and finally felt that I was leaving it all behind. I was as committed as ever to exposing his crime and its effects, but I felt a new inner poise and even some pity for him. I believed he must have been sorry, but was too proud to say so.

"After the shrines of Christianity were in 'safe' hands, many Crusaders returned home and turned their attention to other things, like the cathedral at Chartres.

"How could the same hands that carved these stones and stained this glass have wielded swords and butchered women and children? How could so much beauty and so much brutality exist side by side? This is the great contradiction of the human animal. We can be both noble and petty, sublime and savage, beauty and beast. We can pray one minute and kill the next, create one minute and destroy the next, even love and hate simultaneously. We like to think that our erratic behavior is a thing of the past, that we've outgrown the excesses of the Crusades. But nothing could be further from the truth."

Phil Donahue
THE HUMAN ANIMAL

24

I THOUGHT I WAS SPECIAL

June 1983

One afternoon Karin came for an overnight visit and to celebrate her birthday. Since we were both in therapy, we usually avoided discussing personal problems, so I was not in the least prepared for what she wanted to tell me the next morning. I can't remember her words, for as she talked my world came crashing down. It would never be the same again.

I learned that Dad's incestuous crimes had not ended with me, that he had abused Karin from her earliest years. It began for her in the same way it had for me—only she was much younger than I remember being—nude play, with baby Karin still in diapers. She wasn't touched and there was no physical damage to her then, but the emotional trauma was well underway. Others were present in addition to Dad—my brother Lee (about eighteen) and Susan who was three (but doesn't remember it). They were all naked and the men pranced around gleefully.

Even though the sexual abuses had begun in the same pattern of family nudity that I endured, they didn't follow the same course afterwards. No attempt was made to lure Karin into believing that these activities were to "educate and prepare her for a happy marriage." (As a toddler, she wouldn't have understood what he was talking about.)

Karin didn't relate incidents of private abuse by her grandfather, such as those I recall, but the assaults on her were far more extensive and brutal than any that I remembered. Perhaps because she was not his daughter, Dad became bold enough to subject her to acts by others, which his relationship with me in his "teacher" role prevented.

When she became a preschooler he used her to "service" his friends—holding her down while they orally raped her. Eventually, after vomiting a number of times, she was able to bite the penis of her abuser of the moment, but that did not end the "servicing." From then on her little body, stripped of clothing, continued to receive the thrusts of these sick bullies; raping her psychologically and physically, if not genitally, and smearing her all over with their semen. I can only believe that such adult males, behaving with such raw cruelty, deeply hate females.

Karin didn't say where Mother was at the time the assaults occurred, just as I, years before, hadn't remembered where she was. But Dad always chose his set-ups cleverly and was never caught—except by his granddaughter long after his death, through a process of which he knew nothing.

After many years of intensive therapy, Karin broke through the life-long amnesia which had obliterated all her negative associations with her grandfather and Uncle Lee, as well as the abuses she suffered. Hypnotherapy took her back to the truths about those we loved and trusted—who betrayed us. I don't know the whole story of those years, but some of the details were brought to light through Karin's therapy.

I want to make it clear that although she knew I had been struggling through several years of therapy in dealing with my own incestuous childhood, I had never shared the particulars with her.

It must also be understood that when Karin began hypnotherapy she believed she needed deeper insights into her life than she had attained through standard individual and group therapy. She continued to have difficulty coping with work and the parenting problems she was facing, and sought depth counseling as another approach to resolve them. But she was completely unaware of having been abused during her early years.

One of the episodes that eventually surfaced was the nude play in the guest cabin when Karin was a baby. She remarked that Susan's eyes had what she described as "that look," sparking Karin's lifelong distrust of her sister, which she had never before understood. "That look" implied that all four of them were accomplices in naughty misbehavior that was wrong, but fun. On hearing her description, I immediately remembered Dad's glittering eyes when I was little, and our family was engaging in enforced and hated nakedness. Although Susan was still very young, she was taking her cues from my dad and her Uncle Lee and behaving accordingly.

In shock and heartbreak as I listened, I recalled the many times we had stayed at the Ranch when Susan and Karin were little while I tried to figure out the next move to make in our lives.

Both my parents had always seemed devoted to these children and concerned about our happiness and welfare—especially during those early years. They were warm and loving with them, amused by them, and firm when necessary. I remembered other times when the children vacationed there, while I worked and took courses in San

Francisco or Santa Barbara. They, too, had been unprotected from a danger I should have known still existed, but wrongly, tragically assumed had been left behind in my childhood.

Although I had been shocked to learn of the molests of other children in the family, my father wasn't the abuser and I never associated these assaults with him in any way. I believed I was special to him, and so, I thought, was our relationship. What I remembered didn't even resemble these other assaults, which I felt were only exploitative, not "instructive," as Dad said was his sole purpose with me.

There is a dreadful irony in the fact that while my solo parenting efforts were outwardly being supported and aided by both my parents, they were at the same time being utterly sabotaged by my father and brother.

One day Dad took Karin for a walk. (He was a favorite adult of many children who visited the Ranch, with his gift for being companionable and sharing his many interests with them.) They walked around the Ranch together and eventually went to the guest cabin. My trusting little girl was enjoying herself and did not become apprehensive until she realized that they were apparently waiting for someone. When a pick-up truck drove in, she knew she had been tricked—that again she would have to endure the violence of a stranger against her nakedness, while her grandfather held her down. Her tears and pleading were to no avail; the men ignored them.

Whenever Dad invited Karin to accompany him, she must have suppressed her fears, and expected her helpless devotion to him would be returned in the innocent, carefree fun he promised.

For example, she happily anticipated one particular day because she and her grandfather had been invited to lunch with friends, and she was told to bring her bathing suit. All through the meal while the grown-ups talked, she thought about swimming. Following lunch the wife left for town and Karin was told to go to the bath-house and put on her swimsuit. She went in a bit timidly because she had never been there before, and left the door partly ajar while she looked around the room.

Before she closed the door and began to undress, she heard it click behind her and turned around. Her leering grandfather had entered, followed by their host and, as she said in painful remembrance, "I knew I wasn't going swimming that day." Their host was ready for his terrifying reward.

With the exception of her Uncle Lee (who also abused her), and her favorite Uncle Bobby, who aided him, Karin did not recognize any of the men to whom her grandfather subjected her. But she clearly described the places where the assaults occurred, both on the Ranch and elsewhere. Although she had never been back to the off-Ranch places, when she described them (from her memories) to a friend who knows the Sonoma Valley well, he knew exactly where they were. And when he took us to see them, her descriptions proved accurate. She also described a singular characteristic about one of the men—which has been verified, as well as the location and appearance of his home. (All these men, contemporaries of my father, are now dead.)

Karin's hypnosis further revealed that following these cruelties Dad would inflict verbal abuse on her, to ensure that she would not tell anyone. He would torment her on the way home by calling her "fat, dumb and ugly" and said that no one would ever believe her if she told. All these words describing her were cruel lies, but she believed him and they have adversely affected her ever since. Even though photographs proved otherwise, visual evidence could not restore her shattered self image. More than 40 years later she is still working to overcome the effects of her buried nightmares.

As she reviewed her stays at the Ranch, Karin was surprised to discover that she always remembered the beginning of those times she was with my dad, but could never recall where they went, who they saw, what happened, or even the ride home. Her subconscious mind had those terrors firmly locked away from her awareness as soon as they occurred. Only difficult work with her skilled therapist pried them loose.

While Karin quietly plodded through her horrible story, the progress I had been enjoying was destroyed. Another candle had been lighted in my wilderness of ignorance. It became a bonfire that I feel would have consumed me, were it not for that critical merge toward wholeness after the burglary. But first I stopped breathing. When Karin began to tell me, my response system went on automatic pilot and I felt myself cruise through the revelations like a robot.

As she continued I began to understand that one wound time cannot heal is the one caused by crime against one's child. I know now I will never be "over it," in terms of forgetting it. This time, though, I couldn't scream. There was too much heartache.

It may be impossible for many who were not incest victims themselves to understand fully the powerlessness which adult, former victims feel; their inability to recognize incipient danger and to protect their children. The incredulity of others, though, is nothing compared to my own self-loathing and despair when I learned of the abuses of my child.

Fortunately, Karin had given me permission to talk about it, which was a life-saver because the pain was too intense to contain, and it didn't begin to hit me until after she had gone home. Then I knew a part of me had died.

In talking on the phone to Rachel that evening, I briefly shed the only tears since it began. She was sensitive, supportive and clear. But when she reminded me that Karin was grown up now and that it all happened many years ago, I couldn't acknowledge that reality—I barely heard it. I had plunged back into a time warp with Karin and my only reality was the 1940s—the years when she was being abused. Driving up Sonoma Mountain Road to our Ranch vacation—

"Farther along we'll know more about it,
Farther along we'll understand why."

Shock enveloped me for the first twenty-four hours, isolating me from my feelings. I couldn't express them; I didn't even know what they were. Totally unlike the after-effects of the burglary, in which clarity struck me like a flash of lightning, this time I felt struck by the bolt itself, and as though my heart and soul were electrocuted.

My hard-won, desperately desired love for my father (born in forgiveness) was now shattered—irreparably. But that forgiveness (I now know) was based on mixed feelings. It emerged because I still felt the guilt that I could not think away. Guilt had been my companion for so many years it would not leave me, just because I tried to disown it and give it to Dad, where it belonged. Now in the agony of full truth I knew that my love for him was not clear and strong through understanding, compassion and forgiveness. It was based on misplaced self-hate and guilt. And I didn't realize they were still with me until I learned that he had not stopped with me. What I thought I had forgiven for myself, could never be forgiven for my child.

On hearing about what he had done to Karin, I was thrust back into the details of our lives over forty years ago, when it began for her. I saw her as a baby, a toddler, a preschooler, a primary schooler, and couldn't rid myself of the appalling scenes of the assaults that she endured during all those years. Horror engulfs me as I remember her bright little face which gave me no clues. I find myself asking:

How can I feel loss for someone who betrayed us?
And the answer comes,
What I miss is my fantasy of a caring person.

We had always loved him, each in our own way, despite it all; Karin, because she repressed the abuses beyond her memory, and I, because I shouldered the guilt that I couldn't forget, in my need to believe him. But with my love for him gone, my self-guilt about his abuses of me evaporated—totally—both feelings replaced by gut-wrenching remorse for my child. Remorse that I hadn't protected her—rage at his obscene cruelty—and the deepest, loneliest, sadness for my little girl.

The cathedral at Chartres could not undo the butchery of the Crusades.

All the goodness he did with the rest of his life was only a shell on a rotten, putrid egg. Our comfortable home and gardens, his hard work, the charm and ambience admired by so many, all coexisted with a defenseless child, who suffered alone and in silence.

Beauty and brutality were existing side by side.

As truth broke through—reality hit home:

He never loved us! He used us and we are still trying to untangle the knots he left behind when he died over thirty years ago. I don't believe I can bear to work through any more of them, but whether they reveal themselves to me or not, I know they are there. Since he did not stop with me—he did not stop!

Karin had so much to give—so much potential—and he wounded her as a cruel hunter who shoots lovely, harmless birds for sport; maiming their wings or legs so they can't survive without pain, and can't protect themselves from danger.

I remember his smile, conflicted with shame, when he told me many years ago that he only went deer-hunting once. When he shot his first deer, it looked at him as it lay dying. Right then, he knew he would never shoot another.

How could he ignore the cries of his little granddaughter when she pleaded with him—after luring her with false promises he never kept? Could he see the dying deer in her eyes and ignore their plea? He did, over and over again.

The next day I wrote a letter to Ellen Bass. I needed to tell her. I began by asking her to sit down and then wrote:

"When I was a child I thought I was the only person in the world whose father made love to her. (I didn't equate 'making love' with intercourse. It meant what he did to me.) When he stopped and I grew up, I thought that it ended with me. The other day I learned I was mistaken..."

After describing what Karin had told me and my sense of chaotic turmoil afterwards, I concluded:

"During these first three years of working on the book, I've felt I was slowly climbing out of a snake pit. There were set-backs, but the general movement was always up—I could feel it. . . I felt as though I was standing on a high bridge over a deep valley and the sun was shining.

"The other day the bridge disappeared and I'm still falling. Something inside that I struggled all my life to hang onto has died and it's permanent—my love for a person I never knew—who took advantage of my ignorance about him to abuse my child. He nearly destroyed her and I never knew what had happened.

"Please tell me there are other victims who did not protect their babies. Do you know any?"

A few days later I read and re-read Ellen's prompt and reassuring answer:

". . . You are not alone. It is a very common pattern for women who have been sexually abused as children to grow into adulthood without learning how to protect themselves and thus their children as well. Through the demanding and difficult work you are doing in your writing and personal searching you are breaking that chain of devastation. I continue to respect your courage, you inspire me."

Her words broke my fall.

25

CLUES TO OUR LEGACY

In the days and nights that followed Karin's disclosures, I began to sense a gentle fluttering, like leaves drifting down around me. Scraps from the past, shaken loose by the storm of her crushing story, were falling slowly out of hiding places in the branches of our family's life-tree.

Some apparently minor clues, scattered throughout her childhood, may not appear to be crucial, but taken collectively along with others that appeared later, form a picture of a young person in great distress. For example, Karin almost smothered Bingo, the beloved Ranch cat, by sitting on her. She also began to sleep with her eyes open.

Perhaps these were unrelated to the sexual assaults she suffered; they could have been symptoms of the anxieties for which I felt responsible. But were they in their attention-getting capacity, ineffective cries for help—

*"Something I don't understand is very wrong
in my life!"*

—a help that never came?

Although Dad's abuse of Karin began when she was very young, apparently the damage had a cumulative effect because her severest symptoms began after the assaults were over. Years later, her repeated jaw-locking caused increasing pain, and she sought medical relief. Despite treatments, the condition persisted, and its cause was never medically diagnosed. This must have been another clue, more evidence of her resistance to the cruelty she couldn't prevent: Her jaw was programmed to continue resisting long after the abuses by Dad's friends had ended.

Hypnosis also uncovered Dad's mean taunts of her when she was six. "You're so stupid," he smirked, as she worked on her school lessons with Mother during the spring she was convalescing there. "Susan's much smarter than you are." His ridicule internalized with her learning processes, while it widened the gap between her and Susan.

Dad had deliberately used this means of image destruction to silence Karin when she was little. Although she didn't consciously know where her painful impressions had come from, they had taken root—and continued to obliterate the development of her self-esteem.

I believe Karin's response to being molested was similar to mine—miserable submission. We didn't feel there was any escape, so unconsciously we buried the assaults—she totally beyond her conscious memory; I disconnected my feelings from what I couldn't forget. There was at least one significant difference which may have stemmed from the difference in our relationship to him, and in the differing ways he assaulted us. Ultimately she found a kernel of courage within herself—one that I, as a child, didn't know was there.

It happened while the children were staying at the Ranch after Kurt's and my wedding. When Dad found his desk drawer glued shut, he blamed five-year-old Jeff—who couldn't recall doing it, but assumed that he had since he was punished.

One day soon after Dad succeeded in releasing the drawer, Karin went alone into his study to examine it. Suddenly her grandfather appeared in the room—looked at the drawer—looked at her, and quietly said, "You did that, didn't you?" She looked him squarely in the eye and said, "No." Both of them knew she was lying, but she held his gaze. She was finally breaking his hold over her, and he knew their terrible secret would no longer be safe if he didn't stop.

Everyone continued to assume that Jeff had glued the drawer and Dad never said a word to clear him. The truth, and this milestone in Karin's life, became buried along with Dad's abuses and ridicule of her, and did not emerge until her hypnotherapy. When it did, she was sorry that Jeff had been blamed and punished for what she had done. But in damaging something of importance to her grandfather, she did what she had to do that day, unaware of the consequences. When she later held her ground and lied to him, her unblinking defiance won for her freedom from his abuses and the assaults of his friends.

To my horror and rage, I have learned that incest is not self-limiting. It does not run its course and disappear. It grows and spreads, protected by secrecy—preying on and discarding victims as it goes. Just as Dad's abuses did not end with me, the abuses Karin suffered did not end with him and his friends. Although the active phase of her agony at his hands ended when she was eight, by that time her victim role was so deeply imbedded that she became an easy target for others, some of whom had been initiated into sexual abuse by Dad himself.

My brother Lee was an assaulter without conscience, and as an adult had terrorized Karin when she was at the Ranch. Under hypnosis she retrieved a scene when he was baby-sitting during her afternoon nap. When she went into the bathroom, he got his twin brother Bobby to hold her down over the toilet while Lee sodomized and then orally raped her. As Karin recalled it, her Uncle Bobby was reluctant and tried to comfort her afterwards when she returned to her bed. Lee didn't show any remorse at all.

That Dad and Lee were sick is undoubtedly true. That they couldn't control themselves is totally untrue. The abusers in our family chose not to control themselves and drastically altered the future of a bright, beautiful and promising little girl.

I ache when I think of the clues I didn't recognize, and the many I didn't see at all.

One day I was led to make a stormy revision. I suddenly realized that I had been writing about Dad for several years, and had not once referred to him by the name I had always called him—Dad. I could refer easily to Mother by name, but Dad was "my father"—all the way through, on every page. He had become a distant title, not the private person I had loved. I unconsciously sought to protect him from this bad man—"my father."

I re-read previous chapters. In tears, I forcefully deleted many of the "my fathers" and wretchedly substituted "Dad." Then I forced myself to read them again—out loud—while the inner voice confirmed reality,

> *What he did was evil and cruel and he knew it all*
> *the time. Now I feel the connection between DAD*
> *and CHILD SEXUAL ABUSE! I'm raw inside.*
> *Can there be more self-deceptions to scrape off?*

Afterward I knew I needn't fear exaggerating the truth. I only needed to guard against disinvolvement of my feelings—a tendency that hovered around me for months. Muffling the scope of the awfulness helped me carry on my daily life; and I unconsciously wrapped myself in numbness whenever I could. I needed this mantle when I was away from the book, working on my job, or in the grocery store. But I had to shed it completely while writing. And it never became easier to do through repetition. It was an exhausting process that I experienced in private and fully, every time I wrote, from then on.

Because I was writing now about my child, the anger was loaded with a torment which was not present when I was writing about the abuses to me. Every day I had to confront the inner cry: "I can't stand knowing what he did to her!" then repeat to myself, "You have to stand it, and write about it—*less is betrayal.*" That phrase kept me open and kept me going. Another was this note to myself:

> *Stay focused on the awful. Stay with it until it has all been said.*

It will never all be known, so it can never all be said. But what is clear is that I must continue to follow each clue, back in time as far as it takes me. They hold the keys that will unlock the dark rooms in our lives. And as I open each door, one more nightmare is exposed and put behind us.

It seemed to come from nowhere. Late one afternoon I was in my kitchen, scanning the shelves for easy supper ideas. Spotting a can of clam chowder I said to myself, "With a salad it will be enough, although it certainly isn't a gourmet dinner." Immediately a friend came to mind and I thought, "I'm sure he wouldn't settle for this—I think he's a gourmet cook."

That did it—those two words, *gourmet cook.* I stopped in mid-breath and began to shake, as I heard that roaring, falling sound in my head and felt the quick stab in my gut. The cry, "Oh no! Oh no!" formed inside as it had before, but I couldn't call out. I knew I couldn't stop what was happening.

Suddenly with the key words I flashed: It not only happened to my little girl—it happened to me. Not the same person, not the "gourmet cook" that my father brought her to and who had assaulted her, but the same awful abuse. Not many times as she had survived, but at least once. My mouth clamped shut and froze. But I couldn't close my eyes; I was suddenly transfixed by an image I had seen many times before:

> *The little girl is on the screen before me, going into the Producer's office with her mother. The little girl in her pretty dress and curled hair—smiling, happy and stepping lightly—is looking forward to showing him her little dance.*

It was part of a movie I had seen years ago. When the little girl came out of the office I was shocked.

> *Her face, her little face, puffed, red—tears streaming— I felt kicked in the stomach by the change in her. Her hair was mussed, as was her dress. Her lips swollen twice their normal size.*

When I saw that movie as a young woman I had never heard of men putting their penises in a child's mouth. I couldn't believe what the picture implied and yet I couldn't ignore my perceptions. I was forced to believe it. I didn't know why I suddenly felt so frightened and nauseous.

I have never forgotten that horribly smashed little face; the expression on the coldly withdrawn mother who sold her child for a part; and the fat, bald Producer—grinning in his cruel success. When I learned (many years after it happened) that my father had held my own little girl down while his friends forced their penises in her mouth, the little girl in the movie became a constant picture in my mind. She was always there linked to my own child and I couldn't stop grieving for her.

Dad was always my "teacher." He spanked me hard sometimes, but he didn't hurt me sexually. He just stroked, licked, kissed, fingered—and I just went numb. Since I didn't even remember his erections, I minimized his abuses when I thought about them. It never occurred to me that I may have suffered that horrible cruelty at the hands of my father.

I did strange things, though, when I was alone. I didn't touch myself because I couldn't stand it, but I masturbated the dog when I was seven. I only did it once and it was like research. I knew what to expect. I recall wanting to know if he would be like a person—like a man—like my father.

But I couldn't remember doing anything to my father, to his penis. I couldn't remember his putting it to my mouth while he tongued my clitoris. If he didn't, what did happen? I do recall his positions over and beside me, but I can't remember my head being next to his body. I can't remember ever touching his penis. But how did I know what to do with the dog and what to expect?

When Dad roughhoused with us on Sunday mornings he grabbed us all and laughed. My brother remembers Dad's erections when he played that way with us and let his pajamas fall open. I know I saw the erections, too, because I recall the gaping pajamas. But everything to do with his penis is *pitch black*. It's in shadow. It doesn't return in flashbacks. Just *he* returns with that leering grin and evil glitter in his eyes, like the Hollywood Producer.

To my horror as I stood there in the kitchen, all the images tumbled into place and I couldn't avoid the shock—the truth by inference. Although the audience didn't see it happen, we knew what the Producer had done behind the closed door; even though I couldn't see behind the blackness in my Dad's pajamas, I knew what was there and my terror-filled body was telling me what he had done. Years later a chance phrase I'd heard many times before without effect, suddenly brought to mind my child's abuser and the little girl from the movie jumped before me as she always had.

Only this time when she came out of the office, her face was **mine**—the child-me—the one I'd seen in the mirror in my room when I was crying and hurting and alone—all alone. I was very ugly and my lips were puffy. Now I knew why I always believed I would never be pretty.

EVEN THIS

My daughter
    is five months old. I take her
    with me to a slide presentation.
    The room is darkened, she sleeps on a quilt.

The woman's voice is clipped, rushed
    as she narrates. She has more facts
    than time—
    children in pornographic magazines,
    girls in suggestive advertising,
    in films, child prostitutes,
    children with venereal disease, babies
    three month old babies
    treated in hospitals
    for gonorrhea
    of the throat.

My baby sleeps, sucking
    her thumb. When she wakes
    she will suck my breast. The instinct
    is strong, the muscles of the jaw, strong.
    That first week, when my nipples were sore
    she sucked my finger, her father's finger.
    We laughed, startled by the power of her suck.

She sucks the ear of her rubber cat.
She greets the world with an open mouth.
    A baby will suck anything.

Ellen Bass
OUR STUNNING HARVEST

26

FLASHBACKS

Teenage Karin began crying hysterically when I picked her up from her part-time job as a nurses aide in a local hospital. As she got into the car, she burst into tears and sobbed, "I helped with the older men tonight—Oh Mom, it was terrible!"

Someone made an inappropriate remark, I thought. But when I asked her what had happened, she cried harder and couldn't explain it further.

"Nothing happened, but Mom, I've never seen a naked man before and *it was awful!*"

Since she was considering a nursing career, I was puzzled that she reacted so strongly. She knew she would be expected to care for unclothed men as well as women. But she wasn't prepared for this night when she turned the old man to his side and his gown fell away. *He was exposed.*

At that moment, Karin's jaw felt gripped by a vice and her throat convulsed in spasms of involuntary swallows as she tried to suppress her panic and carry on with her duties. Caught in a flashback (without conscious memory), she re-experienced the *feelings* of an assault—her little child-self forced to take a huge penis in her mouth—and her terror was overwhelming. Somehow she managed to draw on her courage and hold herself together until the shift was over and she was finally in the car.

Incest has permeated our family, extending through at least four generations during my lifetime. It doesn't end spontaneously. The abusers may modify their behavior as they get older, but they don't heal themselves. And anyone who thinks they aren't dreadfully harmful has never lived with one as a child. They are crafty and cruel, without a shred of conscience.

A case in point recently emerged during Karin's hypnotherapy. Many years ago, as Dad lay hospitalized with a broken leg, Mother and I took Karin (who was then eleven years old), to visit him. When Mother and I turned our attention away from the bed momentarily, Dad (almost 70) raised the covers and exposed himself to Karin. She was sitting on the other side, in perfect view of what he chose to display.

As she turned quickly away, she saw that he was watching her—teasing her with his smirk, enjoying her embarrassment—yet ready to drop the covers should anyone approach that side of his bed.

How evil, to torture a child with secrets and feelings she can't possibly understand; a child who was brought up to love her grandfather. I believe that incident merged in her subconscious mind with the earlier assaults by Dad's friends, and played into the flashback when she was working with the older male patients.

Additional evidence of Dad's assaults on small children continues to surface as I write. He not only did not stop with me, he did not stop with Karin.

At the time Beth was born, Karla was three years old and stayed at the Ranch for a few days while I was in the hospital. She later told me that she always had bad feelings about the Ranch, but didn't know why. Recently, during therapy, she began suffering flashbacks of being molested, beginning with my dad when she was very little.

One day during her stay there, he confronted her in her bedroom, took her up on his lap, opened his pants and wanted her to touch his penis. When she resisted, he tossed her down and called her "stupid"—his favorite epithet for Karin a few years earlier. After that flashback, she remembered more. She recalled how she hid behind bushes and trees, because she was so afraid of some of the "big people" at the Ranch. Sometimes she was discovered and molested by my brother Lee and others. At last she knew why she always had bad feelings about the Ranch.

Now that I know about Dad's attacks, I find myself trying to answer the question:

> *Why, after all those years of carefully concealed abusive behavior, did he risk my suspicions by saying, "You can never bring me too many little girls"?*

The only explanation I can imagine is that in seeing Beth's naked and relaxed little body in the bath that day, he was already anticipating molesting her; his remark was an unconscious slip.

I have learned that many victims of sexual abuse have suffered from flashbacks before they were aware of having been molested as children. A stressful change in a personal situation or relationship may provide the stimulus that sets them off, or they may suddenly occur during a television program about sexual abuse. During several years of therapy I recall having only one until after I was told of Dad's molestation of my daughters. That shock finally broke me away from him and released a succession of flashbacks. Through them I discovered that I was abused for years before my life-long (conscious) memory of it happening in Mother's bed. And I began to understand my incomprehensible behavior as a small child, when I began to act out my confusion.

Flashbacks and what I have termed "floaters" are not the same, although both are breakthroughs from my subconscious mind. Floaters were received as a sudden recollection or enlightenment. But flashbacks were a sudden re-experiencing of feelings or incidents. For me they had visual components; I was in the scene as a small child.

Flashbacks were always acutely painful. I could not write about them for days, and most of them I didn't try to record. I experienced instead an inner struggle to acknowledge abusive details, as awareness entered through a replay of my feelings of long ago. They were revealing the way sheet lightening reveals a landscape in the middle of the night, but because they were happening to the child-me the revelations were always frightening.

February 1985

For many years I felt uneasy when seeing Burt Lancaster in a movie or on television. I couldn't watch him, especially in close-ups, and this made no sense to me at all. Then recently as I was lying on my back in bed,

> *...a huge head appeared over me in the dark. I was very small and at first I couldn't see who it was. I held my breath in terror as it moved down closer to my tiny face. Suddenly, I recognized Dad, but his face was enormous. His eyes held mine without blinking and he wasn't smiling. Then his lips moved. I pressed my head into my pillow, crying out in alarm, "Oh, no! Oh, no!" He nearly smothered me as his face covered mine and he kissed me hard on the mouth...*

I jerked awake—shaking all over—disoriented and paralyzed with fear. Even after I returned to the present, I couldn't sleep for hours.

The next morning the image of Burt Lancaster crossed my mind and I knew then that the reason I felt so uneasy when I watched him was because his full, sensuous mouth resembled my dad's. This recognition brought instant separation of the two men who, until the flashback, had been joined in my subconscious mind. Although it was frightening to re-experience Dad's hugeness and his kiss, it was a relief to feel the clarity it brought to me later.

But most flashbacks don't reveal a connection to the present. They have left me appalled, emotionally debilitated, immobilized, shaky and haunted. I just have to wait for the feelings to run their course and subside in their own time. Fortunately, as my healing continues, they occur less often.

Those survivors who are subject to flashbacks know that it's like living on the edge of a nightmare. We never know when another one will overtake us. They permeate all our thoughts afterward, until we recover from the revulsion and can set them aside—another facet of our abducted childhoods.

> "The memory does not come easy;
> it comes with screams that will not stop,
> it comes with tears and terror,
> it comes with shame that I felt this,
> shame that I feel this.
> The memory does not come easy;
> I tell you because I know,
> I tell you because I will not be silent,
> *I tell you because I will not be silenced..*"*

Flashbacks can be the first indication to a survivor that a previously acknowledged sexual molest has not been worked through and is still affecting her. Even after the abuser has been confronted, the effects may still be continuing. My granddaughter Megan's experience is an example of this.

The family meeting in which Kurt was confronted was a milestone in many ways, but it was only one step out of the wilderness for Megan. She remained lost for several more years.

While halfway across the country, attending college, she suddenly began experiencing terrifying flashbacks of that night she spent in the cabin with Kurt when she was ten. Equally as traumatic to relive were the painful memories of his cruel rejection of her the next day.

---

*From "Remember" by Yarrow Morgan.

Impelled toward suicide she sought therapy. Then, unable to continue her studies, dropped out of college and returned to California.

Two years later she shared her hold on reality with me when she wrote, during July 1986,

> "Did you ever see the card Kurt (no longer called Grampa) sent me at college for my twentieth birthday? It was a lewd birthday card. It definitely illustrates the point that he never felt any real remorse or even acceptance of his guilt. I remember how shocked and appalled I was when I received it in the mail. Also, it came with a $300 check. I wonder if he was sending it for services rendered, because I sure felt dirty at the time. Of course, my Mama didn't raise no stupid children. I kept the check."

I too, was shocked, appalled and furious at this evidence of Kurt's disgusting level of insensitivity. At the same time, Megan's touch of humor at the end cheered me about her ability to rise above it.

If he intended to silence her, it didn't work. She was ready to expose him. When she sat in my living room during her next visit, her child-self broke through and began talking to me—as a very controlled ten-year-old. Her words were measured and her voice was low. There was no animation in her tone—she just plodded through from beginning to end.

"I want to tell you what happened on that weekend when you had to work, and I stayed with Grampa Kurt. We were going fishing the next day in his boat. I always liked going fishing with him—he taught me how.

"After supper we went to bed in separate rooms, but I felt lonely and called to him. He came in and sat on the edge of my bed. Then he began to caress me. Pretty soon he told me to come to his bed. I wasn't sure if I wanted to do that, but after a few minutes I went.

"When I got there he was naked, and he had me take off my gown and lie down beside him. Then he fondled me and made me fondle him and had me get on top of him.

"He thrusted at and entered my vagina, then ejaculated on my tummy. I knew I was raped, and I didn't know what to think, or do. It all felt so scary and wrong.

"The next day he was awful to me. He looked cross and wouldn't even talk to me. We went camping at Shasta Lake. He didn't touch me again, but he paraded around the camp in his jockey shorts. He acted as though he hated me and I didn't know why. We went out in the boat, but it wasn't fun. I was lonely and wanted to go home.

"Sunday evening after he took me back to you, he was smiling when he told you, 'Well, we didn't catch any fish this time, but Megan's fine and we had fun together.' Granny, that was a lie and he knew it, but I was too confused and frightened to tell on him."

The time for concern about Kurt's exposure outside the family was over. I had protected his identity as Megan's abuser for seven years, while he had not only concealed the extent of his assault, he had abused her emotionally afterward. I asked myself,

> *How will assaults on children ever end if we allow some abusers to escape exposure due to special relationships, or misplaced loyalties?*

It was time to blow the whistle.

The only way he could have prevented this was by accepting full responsibility and demonstrating it through everything he said and did from then on. We had given him many opportunities to make amends during the last seven years. Several of us had encouraged him to seek a better understanding of sexual abuse and why it had occurred.

But he chose not to explore the issue with anyone, on any level. I'm aware that abusers rarely seek help unless they're forced to by a court order, but we hoped our genuine concern would inspire him. It didn't. In addition to the inappropriate birthday card, he made no attempt to support her healing. With disgusting innuendoes, he even threatened counter action, should she decide to take legal steps to require him to provide funds for her therapy.

To me, this was the last straw. If he wouldn't help her, he wasn't entitled to further protection. It had only encouraged his further abuse of her. My thoughts went back—

> *His assault on Megan had occurred in mid-summer 1974. It was revealed in late summer 1980. And the family meeting occurred that fall. Now in mid-summer 1987, I have to write about it openly.*

When I told Megan my belated decision, she sensitively responded, "Oh Granny, I know how hard it is for you. You've known him all your life—married him—and he's the father of your children. I didn't expect you to expose him, but I just had to tell you about what happened myself."

In doing so she had helped me through another block to undiminished disclosure of our legacy.

> "The memory does not come easy;
> I tell you because I will not be silenced."

"Those who cannot remember the past are doomed to repeat it."
George Santayana

27

VULNERABLE TARGETS

"You bastard!" screamed Beth.

"One word and you're dead!" the voice told Karin.

It is infuriating that women can't feel safe from men wherever they choose to be, but since we aren't, being alert and aware is imperative.

As I look back for fuller understanding, I realize that my daughters were conditioned in childhood not to defend themselves. I believe that instead of heightening their awareness of danger, the abuses they suffered as children generated a sense of powerlessness in them; and fed an unconscious carelessness—as though they couldn't do anything to protect themselves—which made them prone to avoidable risk-taking. Assaults occurred in broad daylight, and the areas they were in, although isolated, should have been perfectly safe.

Beth always loved rock climbing in the mountains or near the ocean, so it wasn't surprising when she returned with an occasional scrape on her elbow or knee. But one of her scrapes was not explained for many years, and I had forgotten all about it. Recently she told me what really happened.

During July 1969, while Don was living with us, the family spent a few days on the north coast. We stayed in a cabin overlooking the ocean. Beth, then sixteen, took an afternoon walk on a deserted stretch of beach—looking for shells. When she discovered a cave, she decided to explore it.

As she stood inside and looked out, a young man walked by. He looked in and saw her there. He was attractive and well-dressed, she said, but in clothes more suitable for the city than the seashore. She still remembers his shiny, black, pointy-toed shoes.

After he passed she left the cave, thought briefly of turning back in the direction of the cabin, then continued on her walk. The young man was ahead of her. When he slowed and seemed to be waiting for her, she felt no concern. He appeared to be in his early twenties, and as he struck up a friendly conversation with her, they sat down on some large boulders to talk.

But when he turned the topic to sexual questions, she suddenly became uneasy. He sensed this and immediately grabbed her. While she frantically resisted, he began trying to tear off her clothes. In the struggle she sustained a huge scrape on her arm. When she finally broke away, she ran into the water screaming, "You bastard!" and rushed toward the waves. He didn't follow (undoubtedly deterred by his fancy shoes), but shouted that he would be back that evening. "I'll be looking for you," were his parting words.

When she returned to the cabin, she shoved her terror down inside. She knew that Don (in his perpetual hostility toward her), would insist she was lying if she told what had happened. So she explained the scrape on her arm as an accident.

Later, when the rest of us went out to enjoy the sunset, she said she wasn't feeling well and wanted to rest. Then she watched through the window—saw the young man obviously looking for her—walking up and down the beach. Still shaky, she felt menaced, unsafe, and all alone with her terror.

Afterward, she had frightening nightmares for over a year. From then on, no matter where she lived, she couldn't sleep unless her back was turned to the wall. And regardless of how much living space she had, she confined all her belongings into a corner—which her friends noticed and she couldn't explain. I noticed it, too, but never dreamed it began during an afternoon walk on a quiet beach—looking for shells.

Eight years after Beth's close call is a date Karin will never forget, July 27, 1977 to be exact. She had to describe it twice for me because I was too upset the first time to remember the details.

After a busy morning in the large office where she worked, she was looking forward to a peaceful noon hour and planned to enjoy it by herself with her book. That day she was wearing a new outfit she had made. It was bright blue with a zipper up the front, and she felt happy in it as she gathered up a book and lunch on her way outdoors.

An early morning fog had lifted and she welcomed the clear summer air—still comfortably cool—as she chose a quiet spot toward the back of the building, seated herself and began to eat her lunch. Soon she was so deeply absorbed in her book that she didn't notice an approaching form.

Then—a knife touched her throat and a voice said, "One word and you're dead!" The man grabbed her arm.

"At first I thought it was a joke," Karin said. "He pulled me up from where I was sitting. I remember feeling alarmed but not afraid as he led me down to the underground parking area." Her mind rushed to Megan in school across town. "I asked where he was taking me. He shook me, 'I said one word and you're dead, understand?' and he thrust the knife toward me.

"'I heard you,' I countered.

"'I didn't ask if you heard. I asked if you understood.' He clutched my arm tighter and I quickly responded that I understood.

"He then walked me behind a car and ordered me to 'Undo your front,' as he poked the zipper tab with the knife. Because I'd been thinking about my daughter, my new jumpsuit and how the knife would feel I hadn't given any thought to what his intentions were. His order took me by surprise and I asked, 'What?' He put the knife in my face and repeated, 'Undo your front!'

"'I can't,' I replied. 'I just can't.'

"It was his turn for surprise and he asked, 'What?' I can remember some fear but I did repeat, 'I just can't do that.' He seemed confused then and pushed me from him. As he backed away he grabbed his crotch and I ran for the door up into the building."

She reported the incident immediately and learned that she was his fifth victim. He was finally caught after his ninth assault. But she "saw his face for days," and the emotional trauma of this took her back into therapy, which eventually led to the trancework that uncovered my father's abuses of her.

One of the most disturbing aspects of our legacy is that its extent remains a mystery. Dealing with suspected, unverified abuse is difficult because no one wants to make false accusations. On the other hand, when a number of clues present themselves through the years, it would be irresponsible not to take them seriously and work through what is known, so that healing may begin. In the process the mystery of the abuser's identity may be solved.

Beth began life as a contented baby with a sunny, even disposition, but became an extremely shy toddler and pre-schooler. When guests visited, she usually hid herself, sometimes peeked around doorways, but never appeared. She also hated to have her picture taken and would cry and run away when someone appeared with a camera.

Recently, Karin told me that when she was baby-sitting Beth (who was ten years younger), she sometimes spanked her hard "for no reason." But when I recall my own childhood attacks on my brothers, I feel certain Karin's on Beth were an up-welling of her anger over her own early abuse.

Kurt also punished Beth cruelly, beginning when she was only two—once he left huge black and blue handprints on her buttocks. Before Rachel was born, he enjoyed Beth, but from then on he often treated her unfavorably, ignored her in my presence, and punished her when I was away. I still don't know why she became the target for his suppressed anger.

She was a gentle "nature girl"—tenderly holding a small lizard in one hand, while playing imaginative games by herself. Questions about sexual abuse arise when I remember how quickly she changed when she entered kindergarten. Her shyness was replaced by silliness, as she became boy-crazy. She would kiss them on the bus and her interest in boys increased throughout elementary school. But they made fun of her and she didn't know how to respond.

As a teenager and young adult, she was attracted to younger boys (and later younger men); but she fled from the friendly attentions of older men. This antithesis prevented her from trusting Don and protected her from his advances, which infuriated him.

Beth doesn't remember who her abuser was, or what happened, but she senses that she was molested. There are cloudy impressions of incidents and ample clues to justify this feeling. Aside from her behavior, which later included drug abuse—her most obvious symptom as an adult was her tendency to let others take advantage of her. She longed for approval, which always seemed beyond her reach. I believe this began with her intense, but unreciprocated devotion to Kurt. Despite his rejection, Beth grew up emotionally attached to him, and for years would tolerate no criticism of him.

Kurt eventually committed the ultimate in insensitivity toward his children, on the occasion of his retirement. There was a full page story about him in the *Redding Record Searchlight*, and Beth eagerly read every word. She discovered facts about his early life and World War II service that she hadn't known.

As she finished reading the article, her face slowly crumpled in disbelief and she laid it aside, saying, "We aren't even mentioned. It's as though he was celibate all those years, and we weren't a part of his life."

To omit the existence of three former wives is understandable, but to assume there would be no interest in his children and step-children—six in all—is staggering! Three of them had gone to high school in the area and still had friends there. They were making a big effort to journey back for his retirement dinner, eager to show their pride in him. He had supported them financially all those years and could have taken satisfaction in this accomplishment, at least. But first, they had to exist. What a denial of reality!

Not long ago, when reading in the manuscript about my feelings as a child, Beth said, "You know, Mom, I had the same feelings you did and I can hardly believe it. When I am reading about you, I feel as though you have been writing about me!"

Dear Beth, we are not alone.

PART FIVE

"What we manifest in our lives
is a reflection of what is deep inside us:
our beliefs about our own worth,
our right to happiness,
what we deserve in life.
When those beliefs change,
so does our life."

Robin Norwood
WOMEN WHO LOVE TOO MUCH

28

RETURNING

August 1983

My book was pushing me constantly, asserting itself into every crack of time and energy that I could make for it, but I was troubled because it was taking so long to finish. The repeated interruptions, caused by moves and job changes, were extremely taxing. And I had to struggle harder each time to overcome them—to resume what I thought of as my "real" work.

As time went on I was aware of a new problem interfering with my writing—one I had heard about, but until then had not experienced—writer's block. Each page became more tangled, more doubt-generating.

Memories of the desolate loneliness that had engulfed my childhood had never persistently interfered with my writing about incest before, because the writing process released and energized me. Now, however, I felt desperately lonely when writing about the abuses of my children. I longed for a community of spirits with whom I could feel more sure of myself and what I was doing.

As if in answer to my need, Ellen Bass had another of her women's workshops nearby, entitled, "Writing About Our Lives." I plunged into the workshop with whole-hearted enthusiasm. Ellen is an artist in her capacity to assist others in releasing their expressive abilities, and in exploring the qualities within each experience that makes it personal and at the same time universal. The rewards were immeasurable.

We were an assorted group, in all stages of writing—from those shyly contemplating it and unable to read aloud what they had written, through those struggling and unpublished, to those published and still struggling.

I didn't know if any others were incest victims, but I put aside my fears when my stream-of-consciousness writing revealed my subject, and shared this fact of my life with them. It was the first time I had dared to do this with non-victims since I had fled the first therapy group (because one of the members implied that Amy could have prevented her stepfather's abuses) five and a half years earlier.

During the workshop I felt a key turning and a push to be open when Ellen suggested that we write about "Lies." I found my story tumbling forth, almost too rapidly to record. When we read aloud what we had written, it was heartening to have my instincts validated through their sensitive, thoughtful responses.

Over the next two days, as our sharing expanded and our intense involvement grew in the comfortable, inspiring setting, we were occasionally hit by laughter—like sudden rain, settling the dust and clearing the air. Someone spoke softly into a quiet, contemplative pause: "You have to have a sense of humor about life, or it isn't funny." Exquisite timing—instant response—one more shared level of ourselves—perspective.

As the workshop concluded and we were preparing to leave, I was feeling a mixture of being tremendously grateful for all I'd received, emotionally drained from the emptying out I'd experienced and witnessed, and the sadness of knowing we would never all be together again in the same circumstances.

But as I put these awarenesses on hold so that I could collect my overnight things upstairs, I took a wrong turn in the hall. I stepped off into space—above the downward stairs leading to the basement. Unable to catch myself, I plunged all the way down, hitting my head on the wall at the bottom.

Nothing felt broken, so I was assisted back upstairs to lie down on the couch. My principal sensation was the memory of helplessness when I began to fall. Then a huge emotional wave began welling up inside that I feared, but couldn't contain. I began to cry and could not stop.

For the next two hours (an amazing time lapse when I was later aware of it), Ellen tenderly supported, encouraged, held, comforted and brought me through it. She took away my fear and helped me let go of years of stored sadness that the shock of the fall released. I didn't like what was happening, what I was feeling and saying, but I couldn't control it. Eventually I gave up trying to hold it and let spill out what would.

Afterwards I felt embarrassed that I had made such a scene at the close of a fruitful workshop, and felt ashamed for bringing so much attention on myself. I was bewildered and still unaware of the scope of its ultimate benefits.

There had been clues along the way that I hadn't noticed. And despite the surges of rage I had previously experienced, there was another emotion beneath the anger that needed release as well. For example, when I wrote about the abuses my children suffered, I experienced an anguish for them that I had not felt for myself.

It took over two years for me to appreciate what had occurred that evening following the workshop; full-flowing sorrow for the lonely little girl trapped inside who hadn't been able to cry *for herself* about her fears and pain and the loss of her own childhood.

In looking back on that time with Ellen and the others, I remember how hard I tried to resist the tears because I didn't understand what was happening. I know the reason I finally let go was because of my trust in her, and her gently repeated reassurances that it was okay. Now I ache for the many survivors who are trying to get well while they hang on tightly to their self control, because there's no place or time or support they can trust with their need to let go. I wish there were safe havens, unrestricted by therapy appointments or meeting times— where tears could surface and flow in their own time, and survivors could begin to heal.

It was at this point that Lynne entered my life. Her daughter had also been a victim of Lynne's abuser. They had both participated in one of Ellen's powerful workshops, "I Never Told Anyone," for survivors of childhood sexual abuse.

Lynne was as articulate talking about her anger as I was striving to be in my writing. Neither of us had been informed about our daughters until quite recently, and we were both caught up in the agonies of these troubled young women. We shared experiences and revelations about ourselves we had never shared before—with instant understanding—as though we were identical twins.

We met whenever we could and the effect on me of our empathy and mutual support was instantaneous. There was no trust-testing; it was automatically present. I felt an unfamiliar surge of courage rushing into my life. Twin-ship with Lynne had cracked my sense of unprotected isolation—even though our homes were many miles apart.

As our friendship grew, I began having writing problems again that surprised and concerned me. However, they were different from before, when I felt blocked.

I began to feel out-of-control inside—and very uneasy. At first I didn't realize that the experience after the workshop, followed by

Lynne's support had released my expanding rage. What I needed then was time, space, energy and privacy—and I needed them all freely available. But I didn't recognize the depth of these needs, so I continued to write in the morning and go to my job in the afternoon. As the days passed, I knew something was wrong, and getting worse. I couldn't sleep and often felt "edgy" at work.

Finally, I was so unstrung one night that I didn't sleep at all. Every time I dozed off, mind-pictures of my children being abused would grab my attention and shake me awake—sobbing.

> *I see several of them as toddlers, running, laughing,*
> *falling down, getting up, keeping going, laughing.*
> *Suddenly, someone unseen swings a baseball bat at*
> *each one—hits their knees—breaks them. Laughing*
> *faces—shocked with pain. Their legs made useless—*
> *crippled for life. Dear God, why couldn't I save them?*

At 5 a.m. I turned on the television and found a program in progress about surfing, narrated by a young man from Australia.

"When surfing and feeling mellow, don't think—let your mind run and your body and board will follow," he said. "When surfing but feeling angry, look for a wave to dive into and go for it. Don't run away from it. Anger always brings out my best surfing. At the end of angry and aggressive days, I always feel better surfing. Whatever it was that angered me seems trivial.

"As hatred and killing continue, more and more people will take up surfing," he went on, "and as they head for the sea, they will find out more and more about what life is all about."

He found after winning surfing contests, he wasn't satisfied. He didn't know what was missing, until he abandoned contests and spent time by the sea—surfing for the joy and wisdom it brought him. He discovered a relationship with the sea, learning how to surf with differing moods and how to make the most of every opportunity.

Later that morning I took my cue from the young Australian surfer. I requested and was granted a three week leave of absence. It gave me unlimited time to experience, to learn and to write.

When I began the book, I had the feeling I might work through the negatives and come around to feeling that I could care for Dad again. Now I know that I'll never reach that place. The rose-colored glasses through which I viewed him for most of my life are irreparably smashed. I have trouble trying to remember what I thought of as the good times we shared, for now they are clouded with unanswerable questions: Were they overtures? Were they links to bondage? Were they secret-keepers? What was it all about?

I know now that there will never be any answers or a final resolution of my feelings. I know that to make peace within myself I must live with all the brokenness that can't be mended and go on.

I used to believe that the severe ulcerative colitis that consumed Dad was caused by the stress he endured as a young man, when he tried to keep up with a suburban-commuter life he didn't enjoy. I'm now aware that it is one of the symptoms of childhood abuse, and I do feel compassion for him as a little boy. Something must have happened to him, too.

But he was an adult when he abused us and he knew the difference between right and wrong. Because we were weaker, he knew he could get away with it. Now I wonder if the stress and colitis weren't at least partially caused by his incestuous attacks on little girls.

But speculation about his childhood does not excuse him or change my feelings about him. I don't buy the line that abusers can't help doing it. If that is true and they are overcome with passion, why do they always plot and plan and attack the helpless? Damn them all!

I was finding my rage difficult to live with. I couldn't seem to tap it all out; it just kept renewing itself. Nightmares, sleeplessness, depression and despondency continued, and time was not making this awareness about the abuses any less painful. All I could do was write as fast as possible, whenever I couldn't contain the pressure. But much of the writing was incoherent when I read it the next day, and I discarded it.

However, I could feel that the peaceful setting of my latest house in Sonoma Valley was working and moving me through my rage, despite my strange love-hate relationship with that area near the Ranch and its love-hate associations. Neighboring Napa County had provided respite from this family-connected pain for several years and I loved being there. When I returned to Sonoma County for economic reasons, it felt like an ominous step backward. I had no premonition the move would provide a crucial step in healing.

I soon discovered that uninterrupted time in the quiet country-side supplied inspiration to improve my writing, and privacy for self-therapy; which ran the gamut of profane screaming—letting out more anger, to opening windows—letting in sunshine and birdsongs. Some times I shared Anne Murray's music with the lovely rural scene. I co' sing along and dance around the kitchen, while my little charg·

elderly poodle Michelle and three youthful cats—slept through these uninhibited releases.

But periodic swings back to "understanding" my father and other abusing relatives interfered with my own healing—they shoved the guilt back onto my shoulders. To overcome this tendency, and to confirm my growing suspicion about the way abusers operate, I began to read true stories about recent murderers. I wanted to feel clear that abusers, no matter what level of crime they choose, commit them without conscience or a shred of mercy for their victims. They simply don't care.

I came to associate the place within themselves from which child abusers function with a place from which many felons operate—the ruthless, cruel core of their ego-centric psyches. Although my relatives' crimes did not extend to killing persons, they did extend to killing spirits—and destroying life's promise for every one of their victims.

A conversation with myself:
Will you ever forgive him?

>*No, I wasn't asked—not once—not ever. He never said he was sorry. He never asked my forgiveness. He never acknowledged his responsibility. I feel absolutely no need to forgive him.*

Nine days later came this floater:

"I don't believe it's necessarily appropriate to forgive the abusers of our children. I don't forgive the Nazis and I'm not Jewish. I don't even know anyone personally who has told me about losing someone in the holocaust—and yet I don't forgive the Nazis.

"My children are alive, but they were cruelly scarred. To forgive their abusers is to extend their betrayal and denigrate the suffering they've survived. It is out of the question.

"If being unforgiving is a mark of self righteousness, I do not shun its stain. Forgiving is for lesser crimes than those committed against helpless, trusting children."

One day I was drawn to a book about a man who was convicted ·rdering his wife and two little daughters. I was impressed by the ···ty of others about the accused, and how difficult it was for ~sociated with him to believe that he could have commit-ious crimes.

Gradually, as I read about the experiences of the book's author in becoming convinced of the man's guilt, I found my own blocks to integrating the knowledge about my father crumbling. I saw how easily an evil, but intelligent person can split from his conscience in order to perpetrate a crime, and how he can manipulate others in order to protect himself.

That book* opened me to a deeper awareness of criminal behavior. It was subsequently fed by accounts of other families that had suffered through having an abuser in their midst.

In the words of Andrew Vachss, New York attorney specializing in juvenile justice and child abuse, "To have sexual feelings toward a small child is sick. To act on them is evil."**

When I acknowledged that my father was not only sick—he was evil—when I saw the resemblance of his uncaring, vile behavior to that of others who were convicted for their crimes, my crippling emotional attachment to him seemed to disappear. I believed I was free of him at last.

One evening I watched a TV program entitled, "Pedophiles—A Parent's Greatest Fear." I sat there sobbing with the parents of abused, missing, damaged and destroyed children as the anger welled up and boiled over:

I hate my father for the way he destroyed the lives of some of my children. He left them alive in body, but emotionally maimed. He left them like rag dolls in the dust, and I hate him forever.
Don't preach to me about hating the sin, and not the sinner. I don't pretend to be any forgiving saint. I can still love others, but I have only hatred for the pedophile father who ruined our lives!

Once again, television had aided the surfacing of my feelings. As rage erupted during other programs, I wrote it out with a mounting fury that kept me working (and sometimes crying), for hours at a time. I thought it would never be over until one morning when I woke up and felt calm inside. Although I was not free of Dad's hold, I had taken a giant step away from him.

A week later I went to my regular therapy appointment wi
mixed feelings. It was a beautiful day, but I was reluctant to go and

---

* **Fatal Vision** by Joe McGinnis
** "A 'Literary' Lawyer and the Nightmares He Writes—and Lives," by Jerr
Morgan, *Newsday*, Oct. 16, 1987.

untypically late. As I approached the building and began the session, the old anticipation, which had been so comforting for the past several years, was gone. I began to realize that something inside me was trying to say good-bye.

I felt that I was ready to stop therapy, and my decision was validated by Sarah. It was strange to feel right about leaving her; after all we had shared for five years of enormous personal change. Later I found that although I had completed a particular phase in healing, the supportive personality behind my progress was still with me.

As I became accustomed to experiencing my inner rage, it quieted down and demanded much less of my attention. And my most recent, reluctant return to Sonoma County was a step I had to take to finish off the inner devils, who had denied me a sense of home. I could see that now.

One day as I drove through the valley that the Ranch overlooked I sensed a change. The beauty of the area was at last separating itself from the pain we had experienced there. I sensed that I could settle down, free of constant reminders. I had stopped running, trying to escape the past. I knew I was coming to terms with it, and taking charge of my life. It had taken a long time, but it felt so good. I was sixty-four years old.

29

HEALING

Spring 1985

As I felt a sense of peace growing within myself, I sensed a change in relationships with my four daughters who live in California. (Susan and Jeff live too far away for frequent contact.) Some of the changes I welcomed—some were scary. I was still vulnerable to any shift in the winds blowing between us that indicated their displeasure. But, despite uncertainties about their feelings, I believed we could achieve the clear, healthy, independent relationships that most parents hope for and felt ready to work with them for deeper understanding.

When I began this book, I hoped that in addition to speaking to older women like myself, it would also speak to my children. I hoped it would help lead us out of the morass of hurts, misunderstandings, anguish and pain that had held us apart for so long. I had thought they might benefit by knowing the process I had gone through to grow up— the steps along the way. Finally I saw that I couldn't leave a blueprint for healing that would be of any value. We each must make our own. And besides I still wasn't all grown up!

Now I believe that healing cannot occur merely through knowing causes and effects—we each must feel and release our own hidden emotions. Each of us is the sole owner of the key to these feelings and must unlock them for ourselves. I can only provide a little light on the locks, and stand aside. My children will have to depend on their awareness of their own realities—as individuals—separate from me.

Ultimately as my children's personal problems began to surface and interfere with their lives as adults, they sought professional assistance in working through them. I was relieved when each one made the decision, instead of wasting years (as I had), hoping the useless hope of unassisted cure.

But I was unprepared to have the same course that had taken me into negative feelings against my mother take them into similar feelings against me. The difference is that I was unable to tell Mother about my feelings and clear them out. They did tell me, but sometimes I wasn't ready to hear them.

Afraid of their rejection, I didn't know how to make amends—so I backed off into my own inner cave to lick my wounds and be miserable. I felt so bewildered and sorry for myself I couldn't write no matter how hard I tried.

One day, several years after the rest of the country had been hearing it in the motion picture and on the radio, I heard the song "The Rose" for the first time. It was being sung on television by the poet who wrote it.

Tears for each one of my struggling, grown-up children overcame me. The message was so clear, the challenge to believe it so pure and honest, I felt washed clean and ready to be a loving person—maybe for the first time. I suddenly knew, as the words said, the seed was there inside and it was up to me to help it flower.

I began to re-contact my daughters, with the expectation of success and without inuendoes that stemmed from fear of rejection. Incest survivors have strength—to have survived—and I was always told I was strong, long before anyone knew what I had survived. What I felt I needed was courage—to look within and find myself—face up to shortcomings that only I could change.

One by one, my daughters responded in a positive way. Some were able to share much more about the sexual abuses they had suffered than they ever had before. It was *our* problem—not just theirs privately and mine in a book. When we exchanged confidences it was on a more mature level, more as friends or sisters than it had been in the past. Recognizing useless, negative response modes, generated from our childhoods, and consciously devising new ones to replace them wasn't easy at first, but it was worth the effort.

One time I wrote to Rachel after we had spent an unsharing weekend together. She had seemed preoccupied no matter where we went or what we did.

I wanted her to know that I had noticed it, hoped I hadn't caused it, and that if I had, I wanted her to try to tell me about it.

She responded in a few days with warmth and appreciation. She said that she had come to see me with an unresolved problem she didn't want to share—knew it was interfering between us, and was very sorry that she hadn't been able to put it aside for the weekend. She was not in the least defensive about herself or critical of me. And her sincere thanks for my bringing our unease out in the open was wonderful to receive.

We have all become richer because they were willing to take steps back to their early years and disclose their pain, as well as address present irritations, despite all our vulnerabilities.

One of the loveliest examples of healing came to me in a recent letter from Karla. She had mentioned in a previous letter that she was beginning to help other survivors, and I wanted to know more.

"If I see a sign, a possible sign to me in another person that I suspect could be caused by sexual abuse as a child, I immediately feel a mental spark, empathy, kinship. I will at the right time use myself as an example to hopefully make them feel comfortable enough to share that they were also sexually abused," she wrote.

"If, as has happened, people don't remember being sexually abused, I also mention how I felt emotionally and mentally. They go home and often think about what I have shared. Sometimes it sparks something in them and sometimes it does not.

"I am immensely enjoying working with other alcoholics. By doing this I stay sober, have a feeling of purpose and I learn a lot about myself and therefore people. Many alcoholics were brought up in alcoholic homes where sexual abuse was present. It seems to me sexual abuse and alcohol abuse and alcoholism often go hand in hand—although not always.

"So since I have had both sexual abuse and alcoholism I can help even more. I have turned my past into a real, positive, helpful tool. I have talked in meetings about the sexual abuse and it helps me and helps others to be honest and not stuff their past.

"I still have some unresolved feelings about the sexual abuse, but I am now less fearful, less angry, less resentful—and I will continue to lose my fear, anger and resentments, one day at a time."

The greatest stimulus to my own healing was seeing and feeling it at last occurring in my children.

30

SERENDIPITY

Throughout my life there have been periods when I've sensed that ordinary events, or apparently chance meetings were not ordinary or chance. They were preparing me. They were forerunners of a phase that I couldn't have imagined: fortunate, accidental discoveries—*serendipity*.

After I returned to Sonoma County, I felt drawn westward and settled in the town of Sebastopol. As is my custom wherever I live, I began reading one of the local newspapers to familiarize myself with the personalities and issues of the area. Soon I began to think of the various local columnists as new young friends, and enjoyed becoming acquainted with them through their work.

Gradually, one whose skill, honesty and sense of humor I admired, separated out from the rest in my mind. So on several occasions I sought his views about local problems that concerned me. Bruce Robinson's direct, serious manner and responses were surprisingly supportive. I knew I could trust him.

At the same time (like the other side of the coin), I became aware of a huge chip on my shoulder where men, in general, were concerned. The ones I'd known best during my lifetime had proved untrustworthy and when I thought of the pain they brought to so many of us, I could feel myself getting bitter. I knew it was unfair, but I couldn't seem to help it or stop it from dominating my thoughts. Except for Bruce, whom I barely knew, I was becoming afraid to trust anyone. It was like an obsession and frightened me.

One morning when I thought I'd hit bottom over this it came to me—

If you stay aware and trust your own instincts, you won't be fooled by wishful assumptions about anyone. You will know. Trust your own judgment, about when to reach out, why, and to whom.

Although I still didn't know how to use that directive, it was a comfort. It took me out of the anti-male despair I was in. But once again, my writing had suffered as these latest disillusions ran their course. It was getting late—years late—and I was getting fearful about completing the book. For the first time, I could feel the spark dying.

> *Is it worth saving? I'm so tired of all of it. Can't I just
> let it die?*

Words rushed in as they had in the car nearly eight years before, when I was pulled toward the telephone poles along the road—

> *No, not yet! No, not yet! No, not yet!*

But this time there was no one close by to save my book, as Sarah had been to save me that day when I wanted to die.

> *Ellen and Lucy are too far away. I can't go on
> anymore like this. I need professional guidance and
> feedback here, now, and until the book's finished.
> Who? Bruce Robinson? But do I want help from a
> man who barely knows me? Can I risk it—this starkly
> candid manuscript?—Dare I risk it?*

I knew if he chose to help me, he would give me honest feedback, but would he find it interesting? Had I made full use of Ellen's and Lucy's critiques?

My father, brothers, and Kurt, hadn't been interested in what I had to say—about anything. The only feedback I got from them was either yawns or put-downs. Enough of them!

> *Trust your own instincts. Contact Bruce.*

So I did. And he agreed to give me an editorial hand. As the Managing Editor of the paper and host on a local television interview program, I had no doubts about his qualifications. They supplemented the qualities I respected him for already.

When we began, he asked me questions I'd never been asked, which arose in his mind while he read. He probed relationships. I was nervous at first because I didn't want to let him down. I wanted his respect, as well as his guidance. But I was never embarrassed by his questions.

I believe there are several reasons for this. Most important—he is a professional. To him, it was an absorbing new challenge and he gave it his best. "It rings absolutely true and honest," he told me. From a journalist, this was valuable support.

Another positive factor was our ages. We are of different generations and although values and perspectives are close enough for us to work well together, our lives are completely different. His work had trained him to deal with everything, as fully as he chose. My life had taught me to deny everything—especially sexual issues. If he found me holding back in my writing, he asked me questions that made me work—and heal—and grow up. I began to understand how writing requires more than colorful descriptions and impassioned expressions of thoughts and feelings. It is a craft to be perfected and I loved what I was learning. It was exciting to feel myself improving.

Someone else's adult son was giving me the support I needed—just as my own adult children had—with his professional responses to my work akin to their personal ones. But he also responded with sensitivity to my fears for the book and need for reassurance. After reading the first few chapters he said one day, "I'm truly committed to seeing this through with you," which was hard to believe, since I had grown to expect others to lose interest in whatever I cared about. Then time and again he proved he meant it—no matter how busy he was.

But before all this, the strongest motivation came from sensing that working on the book with him was the next logical step. I call it *serendipity*, and it couldn't have chosen a better moment to happen.

217

31

NO MORE PRETENDING

Summer 1987

"What about your relationship with your brothers?" Bruce asked, after reading the early chapters. "You have written in detail about your parents, but I don't have a clear picture of your brothers."

I don't believe I do either. How strange—we're all over sixty—and I don't feel close to them at all. I never have.

But I wasn't ready to tell him that yet. I was caught in an inner turmoil about my brothers and wanted to resolve it before I tried to write any more about them.

It has taken years for me to realize how dysfunctional my family actually was—and how every relationship was affected. By this, I mean more than knowing that certain members sexually abused children; I mean acknowledgment of the sense of alienation from a family in which I felt no emotional support.

Occasionally, a remnant of the past, like an old snapshot, will remind me of an earlier time and surprise me with a new message. There was one of Amy on the grass when she was about four. She is holding her little brother Nicky on her lap and their older brother Paul is beside her. They look a little mussed up from playing, but happy and *loving*. Susan's children were good to each other—kind, caring and loyal. When they teased in fun, they were never mean.

Recently, I was troubled by a change in my feelings about my brothers. It wasn't that they said or did something that upset me—it was a fuzzy awareness of the emotional poverty between us. What was wrong? With me? With them? Why now?

The snapshot of Amy and her brothers held some answers. It reminded me of them as children, rolling and playing on the grass like little puppies. I recalled them a few years later when Susan was at work—Amy, smiling but firm, reminding the boys to wash the dishes, while she tidied the house "before Mom comes home."

All at once I remembered. When I watched them together I knew what I'd missed, what we'd all missed. Although we did have fun times as children, my brothers and I never felt close. I believe the boys felt comfortable together, but to me it always felt like "me and them," never "we," or "you and I."

The more conscious I became of this, the more every contact with any of them confirmed it. I began to feel like a smiling puppet and was uneasy about it. I didn't know how they felt, but when we were together, casual conversation and simple courtesies felt like a charade. I felt phoney.

Perhaps during the soul-searching of the last few years it was inevitable that I would begin to look beneath the surface of my relationship with them. And when I did, I saw one more denial of family reality. "Shoulds" about our feelings of love are not enough. The truth was—I didn't feel love between us.

In later months, I found my alienation toward my brothers turning to anger—first at them and then at myself for misplacing my trust. This extended beyond Lee and his abuses of the children.

> *Why did it take so long to wake up? Too many times*
> *I have felt their distance, dislike, and petty disloyalty,*
> *while I tried to overlook their superficial sincerity.*
> *But somehow their attention never feels warm-hearted.*
> *It's more like alms dutifully offered—without respect*
> *or affection—and after I've been with them I feel*
> *empty. I have misplaced trust in their feelings for me,*
> *just as I had with Dad's, Kurt's, Don's, and how many*
> *others?*

Now, in response to Bruce's question, I found I couldn't describe them individually, since I felt estranged from all of them. It wasn't that our lukewarm relationships had deteriorated; they never warmed up. "Am I finally seeing us as we really are?" I wondered. We never were true family—in spirit or love—because genes are not enough.

As adults we played the game of pretending to care, but in truth we never did. Recently when I began to feel more uncomfortable when we were together, I tried to deny this unease to myself. But it only got worse.

Finally I learned that there was more curiosity, anxiety and resistance to my book than I had realized, since none of them had asked me about it for months. When I also learned they discussed it behind my back, I was through playing "let's pretend" with them. They thought only of themselves.

None have expressed sincere concern for my children and their obviously damaged lives. Their concern is for their own children—that they not be disillusioned about their grandfather—and for Lee, that he not be hurt, as one of them said, "because he is my brother and I love him." It amazes me that I swallowed all this hypocrisy, that I wrote on alone—instead of screaming at all of them, "Go to Hell! and take your idiotic family pride with you!"

In the end it is so clear. There will be no big scene—just candid acknowledgment of my feelings. Meantime, there is no loss to mourn. I can't lose something I never really had.

> "What you give you keep;
> What you keep you lose;
> And when you die
> You take with you only
> That which you have given away."
>   *Anonymous*

"It was his choice, Belle. No matter how he was raised, no matter what was done to him. There's no law says he has to repeat the pattern. He's not off the hook. I came up with guys raised by monsters. Did time with them when I was a kid. They still had choices."

Andrew Vachss
*From **Blue Belle***

32

ENDING THE LEGACY

Reality Update

It must be apparent by now that my healing from incest has been a slow, uneven process. Although flashbacks often brought unexpected clarity, some of the insights have not occurred to me for several years after the clues to them first emerged. When they do it's like finally recognizing where a puzzle piece belongs. Sometimes it's even more dramatic, like a sudden clap of thunder before the rain begins.

Despite the evil pall of sexual abuse that permeated my childhood, inexplicably Dad was always my favorite parent, partly because I never felt that Mother liked me. But long after both were dead I discovered that she was not entirely responsible for my unease with her, which was different from my unease with him. I always sensed in her a permanently imbedded anxiety toward me along with her basic inability to understand and accept me (I can only imagine her torture when she knew Dad was molesting me and didn't know what to do about it). With him, my unease stemmed from hating what he did when we were by ourselves and fearing to be alone with him, but I always felt that he cared for me and appreciated me—even in non-sexual ways—that Mother didn't. So he was my favorite parent.

But he didn't deserve to be. During high school when he told me my friendship with Marty would have to end because Mother was worried about me I thought he was just interceding for her—not for himself. He hadn't been physical with me for several years and I believed he wanted the friendship to end only to allay Mother's fears.

Fifty years later at our class reunion, Marty and I met for the first time since high school. His first words to me in private, "Why didn't they like me?" brought me close to tears. Then he asked if I knew that my father had telephoned him all those years ago and told him, "Stay away from Barbara." But he never knew why and I never knew about the phone call until that minute.

I had never thought of Dad as being like other incestuous fathers who continue to sexually assault their daughters through their teen years, because he didn't—physically. But he was just like them—

emotionally. It took me a long time to fully acknowledge his pathological compulsion to possess me, and the lengths he would go to secure his control.

But wait, you say, when you learned of his abuses of your children wasn't that more than enough to destroy your feelings for him and his hold over you?

Indeed it should have been and I thought it had, but it didn't destroy the pull on my heart when I remembered the good times we had when I was little; his care of me when I was sick, or when I saw a young father showing his small daughter how to ride her new bike and recalled his teaching me how to change the sheets on my bed when I was only five. These poignant memories returned now and then to haunt me all out of proportion to the reality of his repeated betrayals.

After years of therapy, writing and healing, an unconscious cord still bound me to my fantasy father and I thought I would have to live with this split in my feelings forever. It was 1988. I was reading *Blue Belle* by Andrew Vachss.

> *"It was his choice, Belle."* (Barbara) *"No matter how he was raised, no matter what was done to him."* (He) *"still had choices."*

Those words shattered his hidden hold over me. Dad knew what he did was wrong and *he just didn't care.* When the truth I needed to feel in my heart came through another's unequivocal candor it was an intensely profound experience—like falling asleep in an old familiar, but shadowy bedroom, to awaken suddenly in bright sunshine, somewhere new and far away—instantly aware that I was finally free and home in Reality. In the three years since I first read those words the haunting memories have not returned.

A Brief Review

Long ago, when Dad put his molesting hand on me—his child— he reached ahead through time to molest his great grandchildren not yet born. And his legacy still remains, partially hidden. It will never be fully uncovered.

I have written about some of the abusers and some of the survivors, but not about all of them; there were several boys among the victims. All of us growing up in three generations of dysfunctional families during a span of nearly 70 years were adversely affected. Assaults included pimping, rape and sodomy. Abuses that were not physically painful and were seductively masked as expressions of affection produced unnatural emotional bonding—a nearly impenetrable block for young victims to overcome. The most painful experience for some was being thrust aside and ridiculed, scorned or hated.

Many of the survivors have spent months, even years, in various types of therapy, working to find the wholeness we lost when our childhoods were stolen from us. Aftereffects include several suicide attempts by at least two victims, illegal drug abuse and sexual promiscuity, and a number of broken marriages. We heal slowly—not steadily—and the scars will never completely disappear. They are a permanent part of our history. Our goal is to transform them, to keep their aftereffects from running us as we learn how to break old patterns and take control of our lives.

For years, Amy's stepfather was the only offender reported to the police and he was not prosecuted. Megan's offender, Kurt, acknowledged partial responsibility, but later threatened her if she sought financial aid for therapy.

The other exploiters have never, to my knowledge, been confronted by any of the victims. It takes so much strength to work through child sexual abuse, while surviving in the present, that the courage and commitment needed to expose the abusers can take years to generate. In response to my remorse over not reporting them long ago, one of my daughters said, "We're all grown up now, Mom, it's up to us." And she did, to the police, in case her abuser still has access to children. I hope now these bullies will see themselves as they really are and know that their "cover was blown" long ago.

I know that this book has caused pain, especially to those who knew and loved the principals. The pain of disillusionment, betrayal, awareness of duplicity, and tarnished memories can be loaded with anguish, rage and heart-ache. It feels as though it will never end. I have experienced all these feelings and I would not wish them on anyone else. But blind family loyalty cannot require its members to protect those who dishonor the family.

All I can say to the outraged, who may be angry with me for exposing these skeletons is—you have a right to feel outraged; and I must suggest that you redirect your anger to the crime and the abusers, of whom I have written.

Use your rage. The problem is immense; eradication begins in pain and anger. It expands through informed commitment.

> "If no one interferes and no one intercedes, the incest family may continue for countless generations, without help and without change. Carrying within it the seeds of its own destruction and the crippling of its children the family is trapped in not knowing and in not being able to reach beyond itself to the resources that can help its members better understand and alter their pattern of behavior."
>
> *Sandra Butler*
> ***CONSPIRACY OF SILENCE***

I have never figured out how to tell people things they don't want to hear in a way that enables them to accept it. But I am trusting my instincts to tell them as clearly as I can.

To those relatives and others who sexually abused children in our family, I address the following:

1) You may believe that you are known only to your victims, but others are also aware. If anyone has disgraced the family, you have.

2) You owe me nothing—no explanations, no rationales, no excuses. If offered, I wouldn't accept them. They are irrelevant.

3) You do owe your victims, at the very least, your acknowledgment and acceptance of total responsibility for what you did to them.

4) All were severely damaged. No matter how well some may appear to have dealt with it, all of them continue to pay an enormous price in pain and suffering for your criminally aberrant and cruel behavior.

Some Facts About Incest

Sexual activity involving adults and children is a felony. Cultural differences among societies may confuse our ideas about the harmful effects of incest, but it's inappropriate to compare our culture with others that may treat it differently. We don't live in other cultures; we live in this one.

Incest is inflicted on children by emotionally immature cowards. Abusers may look and act like successful heroes to the world at large, but in private they are insecure, confused, heartless cowards. A person who abuses his power by preying on the powerless is like a deadly plague which flourishes unseen and out of control, destroying everything in its path.

Reasons for sexually abusing children are sometimes given as excuses.

There is NO excuse for molesting a child:
Not so-called "seductiveness" by the child;
Not curiosity of either child or adult;
Not teasing by a child who is testing for limits;
Not exploring sensations during physical contact or play;
Not type of clothing or lack of it;
Not examples of other abusive adults;
Not peer pressure;
Not for "educational" purposes;
Not loneliness or marriage stress or drug/alcohol abuse;
Not feelings of inferiority or insecurity;
Not having been a victim in childhood.

Any or all of these may give rise to the impulse to molest a child. None justify acting on these impulses. To do so is evil, criminal behavior.

The child is NEVER responsible for being molested, because the adult has the power—the child does not.

Immaturity and dependency deny children power. They may learn to manipulate others (including adults), but they sense that they cannot prevent adults from doing whatever adults want to do, with and to them. Turning this around so that children can learn to assert control over their own bodies, and/or expose their abusers, is imperative.

The issue of power and control between abusers and their victims may be unspoken but assumed, as it was between my dad and me. Or it may be clearly enunciated and defined as it was with him and Karin, because he knew he had to protect himself. She had to be threatened and scorned to keep her from talking. As a child, I didn't feel that I had my mother's support, so he had me where he wanted me, without threats. The insidious damage done by the abusers' control of their child-victims is that it sets them up for the rest of their lives. Their vulnerability to further abuse doesn't end just because the initial molestation has ended.

To Survivors—A Plea

As sexual crimes against children continue, the responsibility for each of us to get our own sexual bearings in line with reality becomes critical. Many of us have been trying to function with impaired emotional health, as a direct consequence of what happened to us in childhood. But the price being paid is too high, not only in terms of our own lives, but in terms of society and those children yet unborn. Trying to forget incest in the name of peace and harmony at home is not healthy. Although it is a typical response, it is not helpful—to anyone—because the problems incest creates won't go away, they only appear to; especially during early adult years when life is full and busy with others. They simply go underground, where they fester and grow, but always return.

Many Northern Californians know that a splinter from one of our magnificent redwood trees contains a very toxic substance. Human flesh cannot accommodate it, so it festers painfully unless removed. It does not disappear on its own. Human children may appear to accommodate themselves to incest, but it always poisons them—sometimes for life. Even with skillful measures taken to offset the effects, their experience of healing is an extremely slow process—never without pain. But unlanced, it festers, and passes its poison on to others. My life has reflected this truth, and my hope is that every survivor will apply it to her own situation.

We cannot undo the past. We can eliminate its power over us and become the vital, creative human beings we were meant to be.

You are stronger than you think, to have survived this long—alone.

You can join the thousands, who at this moment are healing themselves, becoming whole, and walking free.

Where We Begin

As survivors we must find ways to give ourselves what we were denied as children—our self respect.

The abused child grows up emotionally maimed, without a sense of person-hood, without being able to feel whole. A sense of his or her true self is always denied and remains just out of reach—like a young plant eternally in shadow, denied the sunshine it needs, which struggles on, but without its rightful vitality and radiance.

Little girls whose fathers have treated them like adult women partners in sexual relationships cannot hope to feel clear about who they are, or free, strong and fully alive while they are growing up. They have been encouraged to make sexual responses with feelings they can't understand, while they are also painfully reminded of their status as children, through ridicule, rejection and chastisement. They are in limbo—not cared for as beloved children and far from being respected adults.

We can achieve self respect for ourselves through bringing our sexuality home within us—instead of wishing it didn't exist. Abusers, not sex, assaulted us.

Breaking The Cycle

It has always taken more than fear of discovery and reprisal to deter the power of sexual curiosity and energy. This curiosity among young children has nothing to do with morality, precepts of right and wrong, or the rules for socially acceptable adult conduct. It has its genesis in their need to know about themselves, each other, and their world in order to survive.

Some children exhibit more interest in sexuality than others, but all experience sexual sensations as a basic part of being alive, and need to understand them as pleasant, powerful parts of themselves and everyone else. It is the perversion of this aspect of their humanity by adults that merits our active concern.

Adults frequently interfere with the normal development of this self discovery and acceptance, sometimes unconsciously; often through inappropriate responses to a child's natural curiosity and body pleasure, or tragically, by acting out their own emotional poverty—sexually intruding on a child's right to her own body—destroying her innate sense of personal privacy—stunting her emotional growth. (I am using the feminine pronoun for continuity, but it applies to boys as well.)

Although we shy away from facing those truths about our lives and ourselves which reflect our vulnerabilities—to death, to differences of many kinds, and to the idea of child sexual abuse, awareness of its prevalence is finally beginning to have an effect. It is centuries overdue.

I believe that if more children received a sensitive, nurturing education for living—reflecting appreciation for their unique qualities of memory, sexuality, intellect, and emotions, as well as responsibility for their care—there would be fewer emotionally ill adults who prey on children. There would also be more children aware of the possibility of adult intrusion—emotionally well-grounded and able to recognize and deal with attempted invasions should they occur.

> "Deficient as the judicial system may be, it represents a potential limit to the abuse of paternal authority."
>
> Judith Lewis Herman
> **FATHER-DAUGHTER INCEST**

231

The most discouraging aspect of the increase in reporting of sexual abuse to children has been the mounting evidence demonstrating the enormity of the problem. Agencies are often overwhelmed by budget slashes, despite the rapid increase of cases for them to handle. Clearly, the message we are receiving is that a system must be developed to encompass the many facets of the issue as a whole, while providing the skilled personnel to assist the healing of each individual—adult or child.

Repeated child sexual abuse rarely ends on its own sense of self-revulsion and remorse. Its perpetrators frequently expand their acts of desecration. They seek renewed justification and sexual gratification by associating with others like themselves. In some sinister way, molesters know each other and sense who their victims will be. Assaulters are drawn to the abused as a shark is to blood, and victims become prey over and over again. Often the intensity of the cruelty escalates as, in joining forces with another, the abuser drops the last vestiges of restraint on his behavior. He becomes the sadist instead of the seducer.

Although the majority of abusers are males, children are sometimes abused sexually by females, including their mothers. And it causes extreme, often irreparable damage. The *damage* to children of either sex is what concerns me, not the gender of the abuser.

The non-specific caution to beware of possible danger is enhanced by noting that the word combines more precise precautionary words—Be Aware.

I believe if two words needed to be chosen as the most significant in crime prevention—especially incest prevention—it would be these:

Be Aware

It is my conviction that *no child is safe alone with a child abuser of any kind.* Because fathers are often the abusers, and girls their more frequent victims, the necessity to take action usually is the mother's on behalf of her daughter(s). And her dilemma as the wife can be excruciating. However, seeking help in crisis is never a sign of weakness—it demonstrates wisdom and strength. A false sense of loyalty can destroy one's child. It is the ultimate in folly and, with help available, completely unnecessary.

Please, Mothers, put your priorities in order. *There is no real home or family for a child suffering the horror of incest.* You must love her enough to fight for her, if need be. She has no one else, but if you do what has to be done, *you are enough!*

Legal intervention in situations where sexual abuse is occurring is possible, and important. Without this action, secrecy prevails and the victim continues to assume the guilt. But when the assaulter is brought to the attention of the law, the child's burden of guilt is lifted. Although there are still many problems to work through, the first step has been taken, and that can turn things around.

An abusive father being interviewed on a television program said of himself, "Getting into the criminal justice system forced me into treatment—where I had to face my guilt." That can prevent the abuse from continuing or expanding to others.*

I recently attended a public meeting of a governmental commission which had the difficult task of deciding which programs related to child abuse would be most seriously curtailed or discontinued due to budget cuts. Toward the end of the hearing an attractive, well-dressed young man stood up and asked to be heard.

I thought he was a professional like the others, so was astonished to hear him say, "I was an abuser. Were it not for the group with whom I have been meeting, I would still be an abuser." My heart soared at this undeniable evidence of growth and courage. I wished all wavering wives, caught in the heartbreaker that his wife was, could have heard him.

I have to add, though, that although I believe in his sincerity, I don't believe child abusers permanently overcome their impulses to molest. They can learn to control them, but the potential remains.

Anyone who experiences the shock of discovery and the soul-searching involved in reporting a relative's abuse of a child, discovers the heart-wrenching betrayal of family trust that has occurred, and the shattering of family pride. With this in mind it is essential that those courageous, young survivors who bring themselves to the point of reporting current, on-going abuse must receive prompt, skillful atten-

*Unfortunately since this issue has received so much public attention, an extremely harmful type of "fall-out" has also begun—false accusations of incest during custody battles. Although they form only a small fraction of the mushrooming charges of incest, each groundless charge brings enormous tragedy upon the falsely accused and the children involved.

But just as physicians have learned to overcome life-threatening side-effects to the life-saving procedures they undertake and the medications they prescribe, we can learn to deal effectively with destructive abuse of the law. We must overcome threats to due process by perfecting it—not by abandoning it because it's being abused.

tion and protection as a *priority*. For by taking that step they risk losing the support of everyone they have ever known—and they know it. Their desperate plight must be placed in the same *emergency* category which led to the development of sophisticated life-support systems for our hospitals and ambulances.

Since I began to write my way through our family's legacy, communities all around the country have initiated programs to address the issue of child sexual abuse. But they know they are seeing only a small segment of those affected. Thousands of children are still trying to escape their abusers and their own confusing sexual responses, while crying deep inside for the help that never comes. And thousands of adults still struggle to move beyond their cheated childhoods, when their self esteem and ability to enjoy true intimacy was stolen from them.

> "...anyone, at all, can do anything, at all; is *capable* of committing the most unimaginable acts... Most of us manage to muddle through life avoiding the combination of motives, circumstances and opportunities that could make monsters of us. In fact, most of us given a strong motive, in an ideal situation in which to commit atrocious crimes, would not.
> But many of us would; a great many of us would."
> *Dorothy Uhnak*
> **FALSE WITNESS**

It will take courage and commitment to eliminate this tragic heritage, because incest prevails in the homes of the rich and powerful, as well as in the homes of the poor. It is too massive, concealed and devastating a scourge to delegate to social agencies and law enforcement alone. Eradicating this evil crime is our collective and individual obligation; we must see it through.

We must end the legacies of incest.